The Answers Are Inside the Mountains

William Stafford

The Answers Are Inside the Mountains

MEDITATIONS ON THE WRITING LIFE

Edited by Paul Merchant
and Vincent Wixon

Ann Arbor

THE UNIVERSITY OF MICHIGAN PRESS

A CIP catalog record for this book is available from the British Library.

Library of Congress Cataloging-in-Publication Data

Stafford, William, 1914–
    The answers are inside the mountains : meditations on the
writing life / William Stafford ; edited by Paul Merchant and
Vincent Wixon.
        p. cm. — (Poets on poetry)
    ISBN 0-472-09854-3 (alk. paper) — ISBN 0-472-06854-7 (pbk. :
alk. paper)   1. Stafford, William, 1914–   2. Stafford, William,
1914—Interviews.   3. Poets, American—20th century—Interviews.
4. Poets, American—20th century—Biography.   5. Poetry—
Authorship—Study and teaching.   6. Poetry—Authorship.
I. Merchant, Paul.   II. Wixon, Vincent.   III. Title.   IV. Series.
PS3537.T143   Z4627   2003
811′.54—dc21   2003011960

Preface

This is the fourth William Stafford volume in the Poets on Poetry series, and the second assembled since his death in 1993. Both of William Stafford's contributions to the series, *Writing the Australian Crawl* (1978) and *You Must Revise Your Life* (1986), contained autobiographical pieces along with talks and interviews that explored his main themes as a writer and teacher: the importance, as a writer, of following one's own compass, and the obligation, as a teacher, to offer support without judgment. Our first collection, in 1998, continued this pattern, gathering statements and interviews on writing, reading, and teaching. We called that book *Crossing Unmarked Snow*, after a phrase in one of the texts that seemed to capture his characteristic mixture of determination and pleasure in discovery.

In selecting for this fourth volume, we have again found much of the path already clearly marked. In the first third of the book, "Being a Poet," we have gathered interviews, poems, and short commentaries into a fragmentary autobiography of a poet's life—not the whole life, but a collage of hints at such a life. The book opens with his words "To overwhelm by *rightness*," a phrase evoking his two lifelong demands on himself: to write well, and to live uprightly: "What a person is shows up in what a person does." This first section ends with the proposition "The answers are inside the mountains." William Stafford was a sociable person and a delightful public speaker, but he preserved for his writing life an essential solitude and was content to leave some answers buried.

Another group of materials that seemed to call out for attention were his discussion topics, lecture notes, and writing prompts, many of them on index cards, the fruits of forty years of teaching and listening. The book's second section, "On

Workshops and Poetry Classes," again marries brief observations with more substantial discussions. This sequence summarizes William Stafford's approach to writing classes, from initial encounter to concluding salutation.

In his talks, interviews, and occasional responses to questionnaires, William Stafford was happy to describe the genesis of his most successful poems, often returning to them more than once. Many of these were collected in previous volumes in this series, and the last section of this book, "Daily Writing," gathers up another group of these commentaries, some of them leisurely and detailed, and others confined to a single sharp perception.

In contrast with the three previous volumes, this collection contains few medium-length pieces. Instead, we have chosen some extended interviews, for the pleasure of sharing his capacity for deeper exploration along with his deceptively casual conversational style, and at the same time we have gathered brief sentences and paragraphs into sequences. If William Stafford was comfortable in relaxed rumination, he was just as much a master of the memorable epigram: "We drown in ugliness. Art helps teach us to swim"; "Treat the world as if it really existed"; "Any chunk of carbon under pressure will turn into a diamond."

As this volume takes final shape, we are grateful once again to our colleagues Kim Stafford and Diane McDevitt at the William Stafford Archives for their advice at every turn, and to the Stafford family for its generous support and encouragement over many years. We are also indebted to the many interns, volunteers, and benefactors of the archives who assisted in preserving and ordering the manuscripts, in creating indexes and catalogs, and in providing insights that have shaped and clarified our responses to the texts. And perhaps our greatest debt is to the editors, publishers, and interviewers, acknowledged throughout the volume, who first presented many of these pieces. All items not so acknowledged are housed in the William Stafford Archives, and are presented here for the first time, sometimes lightly edited, combined, or abbreviated in ways that we feel their author might have done when preparing them for publication.

About the editors: Soon after his father's death, Kim Stafford invited Vincent and Patty Wixon to help in gathering and establishing the William Stafford Archives, building on the poet's long-established habits of organization. Vincent is the creator (with photographer Michael Markee) of two videos of William Stafford, *What the River Says* and *The Life of the Poem,* and is the author of a poetry collection, *Seed.* Since working with Vincent on the earlier volume in this series, *Crossing Unmarked Snow,* archives director Paul Merchant has completed a catalog of William Stafford's twenty thousand pages of daily writings. His publications include an edition of three plays by Jacobean dramatist Thomas Heywood, a collection of commentaries on poet Wendell Berry, and (with Doug Erickson and Jeremy Skinner) a bibliography of the literature of the Lewis and Clark Expedition.

—Paul Merchant and Vincent Wixon

Contents

I

Being a Poet

COMMENTS AND INTERVIEWS

A Just Right Resonance

To Such a Perfect Pitch

To overwhelm by *rightness,* to do something peculiarly difficult to such a perfect pitch that we catch the universe, understand it, *ride* it, and live. Think of the discrepancy, now, between this overweening impulse and the role given in society to poets. No wonder they sometimes act humble, like versemakers, and sometimes act godlike, like criminals!

The Self's Encounter with the World

The action of writing is the successive discovery of cumulative epiphanies in the self's encounter with the world. It would be too much to say that art, the practice of it, will establish a "good," a serene, a superior self. No. But art will, if pursued for itself and not for adventitious reasons or by spurious ways, bring into sustained realization the self most centrally yours, freed from its emergencies and the distortions brought by greed, or fear, or ambition.

Art has its sacramental aspect. The source of art's central effect is one with religion's and those of other soul endeavors: the discovery of the essential self and the cultivation of its felt, positive impulses.

From a Conversation with Kim

Crows, they say, have a pleasant little song, soft, that they sing to themselves when alone or with other crows. To the world, of course, they go "Caw! Caw!" And they say that when any two things meet there is a little duet—a song of some kind. If you put your best ear forward, you can hear it.

Every person, if pitched right, meets things with a song—a just right resonance.

Sniffing the Region

Being tagged a regional artist doesn't hurt much. Of course the term may imply accomplishment that is worthy only if assessed locally; but being regional may just mean you use references that seem remote and special because the public is elsewhere and hence limited by immersion in a region distinct from the artist's. So—artists from another region are distinct—"provincial," even—but without adverse reflection on their accomplishment.

And in a sense any artist has to be regional. Doing art takes a kind of sniffing along, being steadfastly available to the signals emerging from encounters with the material of the art—the touches, sounds, balancings, phrasings—and the sequential and accumulating results of such encounters.

To look up from the sniffing, in order to find a critic's approval or a public's taste, is to forsake the trail. And that trail is one person wide, terribly local and provincial: art is absolutely individual in a non-forensic but utterly unyielding way.

Anyone actually doing art needs to maintain this knack for responding to the immediate, the region; for that's where art is. Its distinction from the academic, the administrative, the mechanical, lies in its leaning away from the past and into the future that is emerging right at the time from the myriadly active, local relations of the artist. Others—administrators, professors, mechanics, or whoever—can of course also be responsive to where they find themselves: artists have to be. That's the ground for their art, the place where they live.

"To Such a Perfect Pitch," draft for "The Negotiable Poem" (*Approach* 34, winter 1960) and for Stafford's National Book Award acceptance speech (*Publishers Weekly,* March 25, 1963). "Sniffing the Region," from *Concering Poetry,* collected in *Brother Wind* (Rexburg, Idaho: Honeybrook Press, 1986) and *My Name is William Tell* (Lewiston, Idaho: Confluence Press, 1992).

"It Still Takes a Spark from Heaven"

An Interview with Amy Godine

As Oregon's official poet laureate, you must have given some thought to what it means to be an Oregon poet, aside from reading at the festivals or including local place-names in occasional poems.

As far as I'm concerned, being an Oregon poet just identifies where you live. So we say Tillamook instead of Nantucket, but the syllables are surprisingly the same. But you know how it is: A national poet is a regional poet living in New York. A regional poet is somebody who lives someplace not recognized as the center of things. But I don't feel there's a regional voice to my poetry. I could feel at home in New Orleans myself.

There are regional groups, of course, but poets swirl around so much today. I just saw Galway Kinnell. This year he taught at Nice; next year he'll be teaching at the University of Hawaii. I can jump all the poets I know around the country from recollection.

If I had to describe a regional voice in Northwest poets, it would be an adherence to plain speech, nothing fancy or formal, surreal, or overly glib.

Let me respond to that with this little poem by Edwin Markham—a Northwest poet, incidentally: "Someone drew a circle that left me out, but love and I had the wit to win—we drew a circle that took them in." Well, I think Northwest poets have felt they inhabit a sector that someone has left out, but I don't. I feel that directness—plain speech—is characteristic in New York, North Carolina, wherever, *for most people.* So the New York School may draw a circle that leaves us out, but we draw a circle that takes them in.

In "Tradition and the Individual Talent," T. S. Eliot said we need a poetic tradition to draw from. It doesn't have to be the

Romantics; we can follow John Donne. And for a long time poets were imposed on by this. I say, that's not freedom, that's a choice of chains. Tradition today is not one of prior poetry, it's one of communication. One does poetry, as well as prose, right out of talk. You find opportunities and you use them, and if you use them a certain way you have a poem. Vi Gale, David Wagoner, Richard Hugo, Madeline DeFrees—there's a sizable, interesting bunch, and they're my bunch, who are writing talk-enhanced poetry today from the opportunities they come across in everyday life. But it's not a single strand, poetry isn't.

Do you have an audience in mind when you write, some imaginary critical reader watching over your shoulder?

No, it's just for myself. I'm very indulgent at the time of writing. I'll accept anything, any old trash; it can never be low enough to keep me from writing it. You know, the process of writing is kind of a trusting to the nowness, to the immediacy of the experience. And if you enter into the artistic endeavor with standards, already arrived-at ideas of what you want to do, you're not entering creatively into the immediacy of encountering the materials.

It's almost as if an artist who enters into the process with this determination to meet standards, achieve quality, is not trusting the self that's doing the writing. Art lives and develops, it seems to me, by its willingness to risk something John Donne didn't do. It's like Daniel Boone going over into unexplored Kentucky any time. It's all very neat to say you've got to have standards, but if that keeps you from trying a new kick, it keeps you from trying a new kick. That's what led me to say once, writers ought to let themselves write their bad poems. Not bad from their point of view, but unacceptable from another's.

Speaking of which, what are the worst lines you know?

"Death is here, death is there, death is everywhere." Often quoted to suggest the struggle between meter and meaning. Shelley. He has some humdingers. The worst and the best.

I don't recognize the terrible lines in my own poetry. It's something I really don't want to know. It seems like a figure eight in my head to me: to know so vividly what's bad is to know what would make it good. Well, if I could improve it, I would already have done so in the process of formulation. But I'm not all that much smarter today than I was yesterday. A little bit, not much.

So you don't write your books of poems with the hope of adding to or improving your oeuvre, *charting new directions for modern poetry and all that?*

Naw. I don't know where my poems are going. I can't help it. It's my plight. And I never try to be new; that's putting too much deliberation into your art. Any poet who is intentionally trying to be original bothers me. It's the equivalent of tying your work up with a political faction.

I miss that direction in recent poetry. Books that hold their own as cohesive works, like Robert Frost's North of Boston *or Wallace Stevens's* Harmonium. *It seems that American poets today are mostly concerned with single poems; they've scaled down larger ambitions.*

[*Pausing.*] I felt confident before, but now I feel sort of shaken. Because I like whole, unified books. I like the idea of coherence. And critics have said it's a problem with my books; they are almost entirely staccato—conglomerations rather than coherences. I could take you into the study and show you the missing parts. There have been people who've done the coherent books, even recently, and I watch them with a kind of envy, a wistfulness.

Maybe it's part of the fragmentedness of our lives. We don't have the kind of focus Milton had. We say, well, tomorrow's another world, instead of *the* world.

Think of it this way, though: it may be that what seem to us staccato books have invisible connections we're not even aware of that come into view or realization in the writer's life; that writers are publishing, in effect, outlines of their books, and they're not taking the time to put them all together. So back of it all, we may be coherent, and they just haven't invented the overlay that will show the coherence yet.

Blame it on the critics.

That's right, the critics are behind. We're still exploring new paths into Kentucky, but they haven't put it all together yet to find out it *is* Kentucky.

When did you first begin to write poems?

7

Oh, all of us write in grade school, but some people keep it up. I've said this before, but it still seems apt to turn the question around and ask, when did you stop?

As you know well, there's not a liberal arts college in the country today without its slot for a writer-in-residence, and scarcely an American published poet who doesn't teach to make a living. The situation is unprecedented: an entire generation of professional creative writers who hold the same job, poets who've progressed from college poetry major to writers' workshop protégé to college teacher with barely a break. Does this disturb you, as someone who spent years trying many kinds of work before settling on teaching?

It does sound like going down a tunnel, doesn't it? I recognize the problem you identify. It started rolling in the late sixties with the idea that writers could be more helpful to students than critics could be; that someone who actually practices the thing students are asked to do could be more useful than someone who says, "Others have told me this is how it's done."

On balance I'd say I'm not worried. It's a good thing. There is a special hazard in teaching in that it can get ingrown and you can lose the tentativeness you need as an artist by freezing into the pose of an expert. But that's hazardous for any teacher. Now that people with beards are doing it, they say, well, you gotta beard, you ought to be out doing reckless things.

But the poets themselves needed the money! I'm a school person myself, and I do feel academic life can be a home base for all kinds of forays. Chopping weeds in a sugar-beet field, which I once did, is a way to make a living, but the experience is good for about half a day. And you can be distracted by experiences that come upon you not as opportunities but as obligations.

You know, in this interview you've used the word "opportunities" several times, and elsewhere too you've written repeatedly of writing as accepting an "opportunity" rather than working through an image or developing an idea. It's a notably passive, welcoming posture; it reminds me of poets who used to speak of receiving inspiration.

I use the word "opportunity" so many times because I see the process of writing a poem as one which depends on the unfolding of present time while you're doing it; therefore it would be inappropriate for me to use a term that implies, "I already know where I'm going." You can call it inspiration, that's OK. But inspiration sounds like something you can't count on. I would de-emphasize the gambling part. Opportunities are perpetual; you can't keep from thinking or having original ideas. It's like having a muse on a tether. It's just dipping into the perennial fish run.

The notion of writing poems as taking opportunities thrown up by the imagination must bring you into continual dispute with poets who believe writing is the product of suffering, or psychic confrontation or struggle.

Oh yes, the adversarial position is very strange to me. At a writers' workshop last summer, Stanley Kunitz and Diane Wako-ski were arguing that it takes discontent or unhappiness to accomplish artists, and I wrote a poem against it, about climbing a cliff—not just how hard it is, but how much fun it is ["After Arguing against the Contention That Art Must Come from Discontent," in *You Must Revise Your Life* (Michigan, 1986) and *The Way It Is* (Graywolf, 1998)]. The attitude of the arts that you must wait until you are driven to it would be the equivalent in life of saying everything that isn't forbidden is required. I mean, life isn't like that! It's full of spontaneous little activities. And the arts are full of elation and satisfying closures. But I feel coerced by a lot of poems I read today, or as if they're trying to coerce me.

It's that stylish second-person imperative that dominates so much recent poetry. "You are walking through a field, and you see . . ."—that kind of thing.

I think that's a workshop problem. I see it from people who are interested in achieving a lot in terms of publication. Another fashion I see is writers who think anything that happens to them is going to be interesting, who use a lot of place-names, and names of friends. Change the names in those poems and there wouldn't be anything to them. It's a special kind of provincialism of the already achieved, reminding but not revealing.

What's the connection between how you write poems and how you teach?

Every classroom encounter is like entering a poem; you go there and you make yourself available. Your role is to be ready for unanticipated things. It's like starting all over again every day. Grad students want the last spit and polish, but I don't give it to them. My stance is steadfast tentativeness. The students may have written more and feel more confident, but it still takes a spark from heaven.

How you teach, how you write, and very often the subjects of your poems themselves all reflect the same pointedly unaggressive receptivity to chance. What do you think this openness has to do with being a Quaker?

[*Pausing.*] Suddenly you put an overlay on it . . . But it is like that, isn't it? The inner voice, waiting for it to come? If we were teachers who were good enough, or poets who were smart enough, or people who were . . . *welcoming* enough, I suppose we would find good in everything. In every situation we would be asking, "What can I learn from this?" Because, you see, I feel that's where life is.

What do you feel are the shortcomings of your poetry?

What I feel in my work is a steady . . . limitedness. Not enough occurs to me. I feel dazzled by someone like Neruda. All sorts of things occur to him. Lucky guy! Or I read Virgil—a whole book of poetry marvelously attuned to some pervasive metaphor . . . and I just feel intimidated! I'm not up to that. It wouldn't have occurred to me.

Could there be a relationship between the imaginative limitedness you notice and your reluctance to take on an adversarial position when you write?

Oh yes, I feel like inviting all experience to come in, have a go, but it doesn't want to. Still, I don't want to close that door. It may be an angel out there.

Or a demon.

Or a demon. I don't meet many demons in my poetry, and for some people that's a limitation. It's not possessed enough, it's not intense enough. But I'm not worried. That's not my way. If I had more demons, I wouldn't have as many angels.

Interview with Amy Godine, from *Willamette Week,* June 25, 1979.

Contradictory Influences

Two Kinds of Artists or Crafts People

Most of us, by laughing and crying and all in between, establish possession of the living . . .

There are those who seldom commit themselves, though they prepare careful occasions for their balancings.

There are those who try whatever comes along; these are the ones who talk and write a lot. The language bends and gives: it is for travel and discovery. What they say can be faulted—it is like talk, not like jewelry. Where human speculation goes, this talk easily follows. It is the immediate accompaniment of the mind's free flow.

Some people seldom swing into that exhilarating momentum and mutual reinforcement, like walking with pogo stick shoes. Staying with forms that work, polishing their words that are validated by artists—not by the rest of us—they carry on a craft. But most of us venture into the limber dailiness of things and happen with dread and delight upon a shimmer of discovery on every peak—and in every valley—in Darien.

How to Make Helpful Mistakes in Writing

We writers endure contradictory influences that break up our lives. On the one hand we are urged to lock ourselves onto an endeavor that is essentially frivolous—that of getting published. There are those who ridicule us if we deviate in the smallest degree from the straight path toward pleasing an editor with our immediate writing project. Such a goal is unworthy of our vocation. It passes along to someone else the most central impulses of our lives, and it makes of us nothing more than keys to be played by the market, by the whims of editors and readers.

Writing is more than that.

The other urgency in our lives is to commit ourselves to discovery, to follow out our best insights, no matter what the result may be in the marketplace.

Porpoises in a Drift Net

Surrounded by the cloying element of language, there are people who gasp for distinctions and discriminations. One such sensitized seismograph person says, "Every word is a prejudice." "In our time the right eye should distrust the left." We may be surrounded by a system of talking and writing that falsifies event after event, decision after decision, relation after relation. Tangled in this system, we perpetuate it. Like porpoises in a drift net, the harder we try, the more we are entangled. For these early-warning sentinels of language, the punctuation makes a difference; the placement on the page makes a difference; the sound makes a difference; the tone, the pace, the stumble of syllables, the ghostly history of a word makes a difference. Even omissions not remarked on make a big difference. . . .

Tough Art

Certain writers create a zone of language that deliberately offends but stays within its own invidious conventions. Challenging genteel culture, these people attain a swagger, in effect saying like a child, "Look at me, I am being bad."

Indulging in this kind of affront could be temporarily interesting, but relying on it for a main accomplishment becomes tiresome and petty. And to live by it is to narrow one's ambitions, is to forsake a host of more satisfying accomplishments.

These writers reveal an obsession about gentility. Most of us are not permanently shocked enough to be amused for long, but apparently these dabblers in making mud pies can derive a lifelong charge out of defying something they profess not to believe in.

Further, if they can maintain their pose of being bad, they can ascribe any negative assessments of their accomplishment to the narrowness of their audience, and thus avoid being judged on the adequacy of their vision, liveliness of invention, depth of realization, flexibility of language, or other such criteria.

Gaining attention as they do is as cheap as attempting such by bribery, advertising, demagoguery or any other false means. Timid critics help by not wanting to appear squeamish; they give attention to what is outlandish and fail to remark the shallowness of such attainment that lives by being bizarre.

Certain Current Customs in the Writing Community

Find limits that have prevailed and break them; be more brutal, more revealing, more obscene, more violent. Press all limits. . . .

Fascination with things as they are becomes addictive; stronger and stronger shocks become necessary. People want even their entertainments to satisfy their lust for fear, cynicism, and disgust. . . .

We must suspend the old course in current events, in order to protect the young. And even the old, battered, disoriented, blasé, can no longer register human feelings in the blizzard of our time.

Sanctuary, sanctuary—what lives needs sanctuary.

Inventing New Exits

When a writer works he* is like someone who sets himself in a closed room and then invents new exits. He may be a Ginsberg

---

*Some of the pieces in this volume were written at a time (1965, the date of this and the last piece in this section) when "he" and "his" were used without a specific gender connotation, to refer to writers in general. William Stafford was of a notably egalitarian cast of mind, alert to bigotry from an early age. Were he alive today, he would no doubt hasten to re-cast these potentially misleading formulations. We have, however, let stand his original language, as being the words used by him at the time.

and blast out the walls. He may be a Lowell and conjure off the roof or hack away through secret closets. But whatever his procedure, it comes about through a need for movement, not an addiction for attacking certain materials.

The Distinction of Art

Critics, teachers, all of us, ascribe ideas and art accomplishments to various, irrelevant, impressive sources. We speak about the great person who must have produced the book or speech or policy. We are impressed by emphasis, a good voice, confidence, etc.

But the essential element in accomplishment in intellectual things is as simple and unassertive as one of these little balances that weighs eggs. Possibilities roll across the attention, and one goes one way, one another. If that little balance is off, nothing else can redeem the process.

Moreover, results grow from the process itself: language, ideas, the tangle and richness of images . . . these when in operation bring about new combinations. It is the action that brings the new, creative product. We cannot stand back and ascribe accomplishment to anything not deriving from the action. Writing, for instance, creates literature. The involvement of a person in the experiments and other processes of science builds a scientist, and it is action with the materials that results in creative work there.

People are afraid to believe that their most precious accomplishments come from experience, and that experiences make and judge and establish laws, religions, philosophies, and arts.

Being Called Simple

Most of my mental operations might be expressed in simple sentences, I guess, if the sentences were aimed right and sequenced perfectly, with perhaps a few modulations in the tone and pace used in the saying.

If people like my work it is an act of charity for me to feel grateful; my natural response should be "Umm . . ." (If they are sincere, they are not giving me something, though it is true that their expression of opinion may be generous, and I could say, "Thanks, *for telling me.*")

Similarly, it would be an act of spite to blame people who dislike my work. Their dislike is interesting; their expressing it is fascinating. If they are sincere, they are revealing my work and the quality of their perceptions.

It might help to be simple, and to listen.

Here It Is

As a writer, inside the writing, I don't care about the audience. You know, Whitman can worry about it. Critics, embassies, can worry about it. But as a writer, I could care less. You know, don't jiggle my elbow. I am doing something here that you got to get inside of. So I am not trying to create an audience or do something about my time. I *am* my time. And you want to find out what it's like? Here it is.

An Invitation to Alert Interpretations

Talking, writing, poetry, prose—these are all very closely linked, to my mind; and I do not recognize much distinction in the "creative" as compared to the expository, the informational, and the everyday impulses and adjustments we all experience. The poet is one who collects the products of his living and puts them into a form recognized by others as an invitation to alert interpretations. In this view of the process of making poetry, there is no crucial need that the poet be notably sensitive or notably almost anything else; but he must engage in sifting out his experiences—whatever they are—and hand them along in the form of language.

In general, I like contemplative types—Wordsworth, Hardy, Arnold—and by nature I am foreign to intense and acrobatic writers, though I do not have antipathy for their motivations these days. My care is to find as best I can the utmost in relation and harmony between what strikes me as potential topics, on the one hand, and effective presentation, on the other; and my only guide is my immediate impulse, which I try to cultivate in tranquillity.

"Inventing New Exits" (September 14, 1965), from a review of *American Poetry since 1945*, by Stephen Stepanchev (New York: Harper and Row, 1965). Place of publication unknown. "Here It Is," from an interview with Thomas Kennedy, *American Poetry Review* 22, no. 3 (May/June 1993).

Poems on Poets

Emily Dickinson, John Berryman, John Ashbery,
Galway Kinnell, Richard Hugo

Emily's House in Amherst

Her voice for awhile held itself afloat
in this room. Curtains in her presence
represented all that could possess riches
and live so fully that there was no need to move.

Here by the window her eyes received
the world, round and still, round and still
all day till the slow surprise of the moon
topped the outer forest that fringed the horizon.

We have you, voice, in here. The world
it carries has no horizon. Curtains
descend when shadows and evening come
or when any word comes near your name.

What I Didn't Tell Berryman

This note is a toy airplane to fly
out over the freezing water and land
evenly, dragging itself away from your hand,
one of the things you couldn't quite have.

"We waited awhile," this quick, brave,
skimming note says, "but sympathy can be too kind—
we forgot that." You used up many a friend.
It gets deep after awhile.

It gets deep. And all your demands.
You changed the time too often. Now we've changed
the place. And it's not here, this farewell
is to tell you. And you'll never know where.

Ashbery

Where some people live the wires run
underground. Sometimes they come up and
sometimes—no need to tell you this—they don't,
or at least not where you are at the time.
In a world this big almost anything can
happen, or almost happen, exploring upward,
beyond. Finally you know this.

Then when a bell rings, not your summons
but creating a hollow in which you can decide
whether to listen any more or just live,
you think you'll just live but remember how
it was when listening was needed because
maybe the bell wouldn't ring.

Galway's New Poem

Close, where the unborn eyes begin to swim
their place toward the welt or the rose
that will wake them in the poor brute sway
of the animal gesturing with our hands,
we all begin. Back there in the sheath
every part mumbles its name and its ancestry
of liquids and intense, improvised certainty.

A father takes his new baby into his hands
and paces backward and forward for days,
for a year, in his car, his job, the way
he turns his head: his breath finds our way,
parts of the breathing word we all speak
        in this endless hall.

In Hugo Country

There are places on the earth, names
blown open by stories of terror that
still echo and rumble. Trees
lean away, rocks gather themselves
into even more silence.

There are people who yearn for these places,
travel deserts to stand alone
wherever these legends have devastated
an area. Something hovers like a negative
blessing in that still air.

If we can bathe in fire, share
other people's worst, and gather into ourselves
their failure and woe, then in turn
our own great unspoken burdens
may find with theirs a home.

"Emily's House in Amherst" (1988), unpublished; "What I Didn't Tell
Berryman" (1985), from *New York Quarterly* and *Hearing Voices* (Salem,
Ore.: Willamette University, 1991); "Ashbery" (1986), from *Jeopardy;*
"Galway's New Poem" (1969), from *Tennessee Poetry Journal;* "In Hugo
Country" (1986), from *Arnazella's Reading List.*

The Art of Poetry

The Paris Review *Interview with William Young*

In his essay on James Wright, Richard Hugo wrote, "The luckiest thing that ever happened to me was the obscurity I wrote in for many years." Do you feel similarly about your own late-blooming career as a poet?

I think I understand what Hugo was getting at: that you are ambitious when you start and if you have a whiff of success you try to rush things; for publication's sake you try to rush it all the more; then the ordinary slumps in popularity and intervals when you're not publishing become overwhelming simply because you haven't gotten used to doing what you have to do as a writer: write day in and day out no matter what happens.

In your poem "A Living," you write there is "a way to act human in these years the stars / look past." What kept you from responding in more extreme ways . . . did you feel like the stars were looking past you during certain years?

In that poem at least I was thinking about the feelings many people have of tension, of questioning about survival, of the hovering of the atom bomb, all kinds of disquiets that people have in our times. I think I was referring to that more than to my personal experience. In fact, I had early and sustained publication, every bit that I deserved. I never did feel left out for any reason. I felt pretty lucky.

In another essay, Hugo places you among writers he labels "Snopeses," a reference to the Yoknapatawpha County family from Faulkner. These writers, he speculates, are basically outsiders and thus are afraid success will cause them to lose touch with other outsiders.

I understand Hugo's impulse to stay in touch with outsiders. He was a natural outsider. But on the other hand he couldn't *be* an outsider; he was taken in by everybody; they loved him. He was addicted to sociability, helplessly social. And he was addicted to or available to the heartiness of interchange among writers. He enjoyed company and sympathy and liked to extend sympathy. He especially valued that feeling of kinship with people who were failures or outsiders. My own feeling is that I'm not sure what being an outsider amounts to. Maybe some of us *should* be outsiders. I'm not sure by any means that I deserve to be an insider, whatever that would be. Maybe one feels neglected only if one has an opinion of one's rightful place, and I don't have that opinion. That's up to the world.

Have many of your friends been writers?

Not very many. Because of living so long and traveling around I've met many writers, and I enjoy meeting them. Hugo is an example. He used to come and stay at our house. We were always delighted to have him. But in my daily life I don't live in proximity with, or in daily, person-to-person communication with, writers at all. When I write, writers don't see what I write, only editors. My family doesn't see it either.

So you don't exchange poems with writers?

No. Well, it's possible. Hugo has actually written me, in the breezy way he had of ending a letter, "What does the earth say, oh sage?" I would always write back to him. In one particular poem, "The earth says have a place . . . ," I took up the challenge. But that was very rare.

In Response to a Question

The earth says have a place, be what that place
requires; hear the sound the birds imply
and see as deep as ridges go behind
each other. (Some people call their scenery flat,
their only picture framed by what they know:
I think around them rise a riches and a loss
too equal for their chart—but absolutely tall.)

The earth says every summer have a ranch
that's minimum: one tree, one well, a landscape
that proclaims a universe—sermon
of the hills, hallelujah mountain,
highway guided by the way the world is tilted,

reduplication of mirage, flat evening:
a kind of ritual for the wavering.

The earth says where you live wear the kind
of color that your life is (gray shirt for me)
and by listening with the same bowed head that sings
draw all into one song, join
the sparrow on the lawn, and row that easy
way, the rage without met by the wings
within that guide you anywhere the wind blows.

Listening, I think that's what the earth says.

There's a sense of being at home in the world in your poems. And you've said as much explicitly. The insecurities many writers seem to feel, especially in the twentieth century, seem somewhat absent from your work.

I do feel at home in the world. I have genuinely felt throughout my life a sense that any acceptance of what I write is a bonus, a gift from other people. It's not something that's due me. When any editor has a place for some of my work, that's fine, but I always send that stamped return envelope. I'm genuinely ready for those rejections. I've always felt that an editor's role is to get the best possible material for the readers of the publication, not to serve the writer, not at all. If they don't want it, I don't want them to have it. So I never have felt that I needed to push this stuff into the world. If it's invited in, then it will come in. If it's not invited in, fine, it will live at home.

Did you always have this sense of belonging to the world? On more than one occasion you've referred to a certain moment riding a bicycle out to the Cimarron River . . .

Yes, occasions like that. It was an occasion for the free, clear realization of this prevalent feeling I had. My parents welcomed me; our towns were good places; I liked my teachers; I went to whatever church was around—for the sociability mostly, but also because I took seriously what they were doing. It was only after I was a graduate student, maybe beyond graduate school, that I took seriously writers like Sherwood Anderson who were writing about the desperation of the small town. I never felt that. I thought that was the way everybody lived.

Why do you take such an optimistic view? We know what can go on in small American towns—bleak things.

Optimistic? My view of the small town is realistic, at least it is to me. Every town had great views, an arch of clear sky, a wonderful variety of people, fascinating things going on all the time. And in every town we lived in, there was one great big door ready to open for anyone—the library. And I never met a library I didn't like.

Weren't the times in Kansas during the depression, when your family had to move around a good deal, difficult for you?

Well, it was tough in the sense that my father didn't have a job, and we didn't know what we were going to do. We were living partly on what I could earn selling papers and so on, but so far as I could tell that was what being a human being was. I don't know how to get this directly and simply enough, but if you think about it, lots of human beings work in the sugar-beet fields, which I did. And I was one of them. You know, you could always crawl into the shade. You had lunch, maybe a peanut-butter and jelly sandwich—delicious. The feeling of being alive and relishing your food and drink and company is available anywhere. Some of the most hilarious moments of my life took place while I was interned at a camp for conscientious objectors. Someone would get a box of brownies from home or something, and it was a banquet.

Even though you liked the place where you grew up, you left home eventually.

Oh well, I went to other places because I was forced to: I was drafted; they made me go. It took World War II to get me out of Kansas. I was going to the University of Kansas graduate school, and the draft board said, "Go." First Arkansas, then California, then Illinois, and it ended by my traveling a lot, yes. I'm an illustration of Newton's laws: the object at rest tends to stay at rest, unless compelled by some energy to go elsewhere.

Why did you become a conscientious objector?

Strangely, I didn't become one; I always was one. I thought all right-thinking people would behave that way. In those days, the 1930s, the peace movement was strong in America. In fact, Franklin Roosevelt, to get elected, had to promise, "No war." The other people changed, and I was surprised. I thought a commitment was a commitment. There were peace people everywhere, in all countries, and I was not about to break ranks with that worldwide fellowship.

In your book Down in My Heart, *you write out of a need to continue a conversation with George, a conscientious objector you knew who wound up in prison because of his beliefs. Do you generally feel as though you're entering into some sort of conversation when you write?*

I do often feel that kind of connection with the reader. I like being straight across from the reader, communicating with a peer—not preaching to someone or worshipping someone, but talking to an equal. I don't want to give the impression that this is something I've elected. I just feel that way. I feel the possibility of resentment if I'm demeaned by talking up to someone. And I am apprehensive about patting people on the head. Instead, it's a back and forth with the people in your town, in your street, in the field where you're working, or the camp where you are. Just this afternoon my son, Kim, was talking about the ethical problems of writing a nonfiction piece about another person. I wanted to interrupt and say the obligation I feel is to the people I'm writing *to*. I don't feel the need to be as careful about people I'm writing about, though it would disquiet me if I were putting out advice or signals that led someone into ways of life I would consider harmful to them or to others. It would make a difference to me.

Do you have a sense of conversing with dead poets?

No, I don't. I converse with live poems. It doesn't make any difference—it sounds like a brutal thing—to me whether the authors are alive or dead. It's their poems I'm reading. Thomas Hardy and Wordsworth are appealing to me, and I feel that I am in their presence. I read the best I can get wherever it is. I don't care how long ago it was written.

You don't feel a sense of competition with writers you read?

No, it's not like that. We all seek out the kind of reading that we are available for, that we are capable of. There are writers from whose work I get only a very thin part of the signal; I'm not getting the full treatment when I read Pascal or Descartes, but I have a taste for it . . .

In an early poem of yours, "Bi-Focal," you write, "So, the world happens twice— / once what we see it as; / second it legends itself / deep, the way it is." Does a good poem, to your mind, give us something of both happenings—that surface and that deep or philosophical side?

I certainly hadn't thought of it in such a neatly categorical way, but I think that's right. The appetite for reading or listening or learning—seeking out meanings—is an attempt to get beyond superficial, beyond appearances, to realize what is significant. The senses are fallible, and of course our minds are fallible, and I don't have the belief in my ability or anyone's ability to get very far beyond appearances, but again, I have the appetite for it . . . like, I don't think we ever find out what things are really like, but trying to get nearer is a hunger.

To what extent do religious beliefs influence your work? Do you consider yourself a Christian poet?

I might describe myself as a religious poet whose vocabulary, reference points and surrounding culture are phrased in Christian terms. I think I would be whatever religion there was in the society around me; it's not the local content of the religion that possesses me, but the general attitude, the way of living that recognizes more than we know.

There's a great sense of space in your poems. Would you trace that to growing up in Kansas?

I sometimes have thought about that, yes. In our world at least half the world was sky; that is the way I've sometimes phrased it to myself. I mean, there's the land, but it isn't as big as the sky. Someone told me a wonderful story about a woman who came out from Nebraska and wanted to see the Pacific Ocean. The motel person said, "Yes, you can see it if you walk down to the end of the road." This visitor stood there a few moments on the beach, and then walked back, and the motel person said, "What do you think of it?" And she said, "Well, it's all right, but I can't help but think it isn't as big as I thought it would be." This was the Pacific Ocean! Well, she was from Nebraska. I know about that. That's the biggest thing there is—the sky! It's there, and it's an abiding puzzle, presence and invitation.

To what extent is poetry autobiographical?

It doesn't seem to me that my own poems are at all reliable as links to the events of my life. Anyone's poetry could give clues to the writer's life, to the writer's way of living, to general tendencies and attitudes. As the years go by, I sense whole phases of life getting themselves woven into my writing, like a tide: waves are chance things, but the tide has whelming significance.

Are there aspects of your childhood that you think may have contributed to your becoming a poet?

There are emblematic things. For instance, my father worked for the telephone company. He told me about hearing, when he was a kid, that there was a new invention that enabled you to talk to someone far away. And he climbed up on the roof of his family's house and called out to people far away—trying to do long distance without the telephone. It was only much later that I thought that's a wonderful sort of symbol for his attempt to get in touch. I had the same feeling. You know, I'd like to get up on the roof of the house—sort of like the barbaric yawp—to get in touch. My father had that feeling and that confidence—misplaced maybe—but he had it and I had it too. Stanley Kunitz once said to me that he had advised Robert Lowell not to go to the White House when Johnson was president, and I think Stanley saw a little flickering expression on my face while he was talking. So he said, "You wouldn't go, would you, Bill?" And I said, "Yes, I'd *like* to talk to Johnson." I had the feeling of confidence that the language can take us somewhere. I would talk to anyone willing to talk.

Do you think the poetic line in America is somewhat more horizontal than vertical, that there's openness and expansiveness which is distinctly American?

I'm not sure I'm following you on this but I'd like to try. The resources in language and the adventures in writing are available to us—I don't want to echo Wordsworth on this—in the language we use every day, though it is not necessarily that of ordinary people in whatever circle we inhabit. We may not be with ordinary people (I'd like to be with extraordinary people, myself), but it would be the language they use not when they are writing but when they are talking, when they are saying things like, "Pass the butter." Bonuses in language are not literary bonuses; they are available to everyone who flourishes the language every day with people who are their peers in conversation. It would be a mistake to try to heighten or lower my place in the language that comes to me. Instead, I try to accept whatever fluency and fluidity is possible at my level of understanding with my kind of people. To do it artificially, to try to hype myself into being a better writer by doggedly reading better literature, is also a mistake. I learn to use the language by the pleasures it gives me when I am able to swim in it or maneuver in it or interchange in it with the people around me.

Another Northwest writer, Raymond Carver, is known as someone who has written about the people around him, the people he grew up with, and is considered something of a "poet of the ordinary." Do you think there's anything to growing up west of the Mississippi that encourages such an approach?

I know Raymond Carver's work very well and I knew him, and I see the point of what you're saying, but I have a feeling that Carver was deliberately—when you consider his ability—doing the language of partly handicapped people, of people who were limited in their understanding. This was his genius; he got the poignancy of their lives out of the level of language. But as for myself, I would like to associate the degree of fluency in language that I'm capable of. I'm not looking for literary effects by cultivating a language from above. I'm looking for straight-across communication, as I said before.

Not cultivated from below either.

Nor from below. I got a charge out of some of Raymond Carver's writing, but I don't feel comfortable myself in cultivating the language of a group I'm not naturally with.

Do you feel a special affinity for a certain poetic tradition?

I suppose so. Generally, I like a tradition that is fairly serious, that is sustained . . . strangely, in view of my own production, I like big works. I like long things. Most influential for me has been prose. All kinds of big prose things. I worshipped George Eliot. I like big novels. And I like nineteenth-century British novels very well. Starting with Sir Walter Scott.

Why have you never taken on a long poem?

All of my writings are one long production. I break off pieces, smaller or larger, and send them out. Sometime I will get around to welding the pieces together. It's as if I'm distracted in building a big house; I hurry over to prop up a wall with one piece of writing, then have to drop everything to save a joist somewhere else. This is just the feeling I have, not a claim. I'd like to connect big pieces together and have epics.

In your own reading do you often return to poets of the nineteenth century?

I can't say that I have recently. When I was starting to teach, say in the fifties, I had a volume of the collected works of Wordsworth that I read religiously from end to end, including the prose. And got a lot out of it. I liked it. I loved it in fact. But I've read so many of those nineteenth-century poets that I've gone on to other things these days.

Are there any American writers you are especially fond of?

The short answer has to be, No. For some reason, I find myself (except for rapid scanning of many current things) attracted to distant and often past writers—Kierkegaard, Pascal, Nietzsche, George Eliot, Jane Austen, Tolstoy. A good thing about reading is that you can rove. You don't have to be provincial, no matter where you live.

Do you see yourself in a particular line, in a naturalistic or romantic tradition?

I can't tell. Could be. But I feel enticed by all kinds of topics. I don't feel as though I'm in a bag.

You've said you believe that language is social. Is this related to your interest in Wittgenstein's ideas about language?

Oh yes, everything makes a difference in reading: the kind of ink it's in, where it starts on the page, everything. I feel like a scanner programmed to pick up whatever is on the page when I read. Wittgenstein has an abiding interest in language, so it's natural that a writer would be interested in what he said. I certainly am. But that's just as a human who is curious. I don't read these people in order to write. I don't believe in reading so that I'll be well-read and a better writer. It seems a fake thing to me to read a novel in order to become a better writer. It turns into something that's not a novel. Besides, a novel is something you read by your appetite. That has to be true for anything I read; if I don't have an appetite for it, then it's not for me. I don't do it as a duty. And I don't want anyone to read me as a duty, for heaven's sake.

Quite a lot of attention has been paid recently to Northwestern writers such as yourself, Carver, Hugo. Was Robin Skelton's Five Poets of the Pacific Northwest *a catalyst in bringing attention to writers from this region of the country?*

When that book came out I was glad to be one of the five and felt good about the others who were in the book. On the other hand, I think the book itself was probably more of a recognition of something that had already happened; it didn't bring anything new to pass. In some ways it was a long-overdue book. That sounds grandiose, but it didn't occur to me at the time that it was going to do anything special for us anywhere else but in that region.

Do you think there is an accounting for the Northwest renaissance of the last twenty-five years or so?

I don't have a feeling either of renaissance or its opposite. Our country is so fluid for travel and access that a regional recognition is more a matter of convenience than it is any kind of valid movement. There are simply more people in the Northwest than there used to be, so there are probably a few more writers.

So you don't think there's a special meditative quality to the Northwest that might contribute to writing?

Well, I have to take a breath when I respond to that because I don't like to plunge into water I haven't checked the depth of. As a matter of fact, I *don't* think there is anything especially meditative about Northwest writing. But maybe I'm so near to it that I don't feel the current; I just go bobbing along with everybody else.

Did you feel Theodore Roethke's influence once you moved to Oregon?

Strangely, it's hard enough for me to be definite about that. It was only later, after I'd been writing for a long time, that I read any Theodore Roethke at all. He was influential with so many at the University of Washington, and it's assumed that everybody in the Northwest is influenced by Roethke. I guess I sort of sneaked in by the side door and didn't know what was going on.

Do you see his influence in the work of other Northwest writers?

Many do tell me they are influenced by him. Surely Roethke must have given people around him a surge of confidence and ambition about the language, about how it can dance and live by extreme claims of relationship and feelings.

Did you get to know him?

I met him a couple of times; you know, short conversations.

Were your years at the University of Iowa the first time you were among a group of writers?

Yes, I had always been interested in reading and writing and had met writers, but I can't remember people other than newspaper reporters and a few teachers who were regular writers. I wasn't really in a community of writers until I reached Iowa.

Was that a good two years?

I liked it. I always say, "I served happy time at Iowa." It was rich with a variety of writers. We were made to feel that writing was a worthy thing to do. That was most encouraging. I've heard many kinds of reactions to Iowa, but my own reaction was quite positive. I enjoyed it.

It wasn't too incestuous? Everyone wasn't expected to write a certain kind of poem?

Well, it was only later that I began to hear that that was what happened. That happens at any writers' colony, where people influence each other. Looking back, I do see in the workshop there were certain prevalent opinions, but they were not by any means Paul Engle's. There were others there who were quite opinionated.

I remember a statement of yours about not being interested in master-disciple relationships.

Yes, I have a feeling that art is something you do yourself, and that any time you turn the decisions over to someone else you're postponing, at best, your own development. The atmosphere of the workshop should be that of trying out one's own work and accepting the signals from others but not accepting the dictation of others because that is a violation of the spirit of art. Art can't be done by somebody else, it has to be done by the artist.

Has Oregon been a good place for you? A good place to get your work done?

I think it has been a fine place for me. I have no negatives about it: I even like the rain. But it's also been good in the way that obscurity was good for Hugo. Whenever I've traveled to a place where there are many writers and the reverberation is intense—say New York City—I have felt some need to get away. It is just that if I stayed, my urge toward sociability would lead to many distractions. In the Northwest you're at Yaddo all the time. You don't have to get a grant to be in a place where you won't be troubled by the distractions. Some writers feel they have to escape to this by getting a grant. I hope this doesn't divert any money from the Northwest, but that's a feeling of mine: being in the Northwest is like one long Guggenheim.

Even more than sight, sound seems central to your poems, for instance in "Owls at the Shakespeare Festival." Is there a relation between sight and distraction?

Owls at the Shakespeare Festival

How do owls find each other
in the world? They fly the forest
calling, "Darling, Darling."

Each time the sun goes out a world
comes true again, for owls:
trees flame their best color—dark.

At Shakespeare once, in Ashland,
when Lear cried out, two owls
flared past the floodlights:

On my desk I keep a feather
for those far places thought
fluttered when I began to know.

Yeah, that's interesting to me. Sound is something I'm very conscious of. And maybe that's part of the Northwest; there is a mossy, drenched sound here. So you listen more carefully; you're an owl. You don't have to put on earmuffs to keep from damaging your hearing. It's nice and quiet, so you listen. But in a way that's a metaphor too. It is an alertness of sense in a world where senses are never enough—any of the senses. I thought maybe you were going to say smell. I feel I'm really a good smeller, and I value that, though on the other hand, I look at a bloodhound and realize I've got a ways to go. So, whatever the senses in my poems, I am consciously aware of the limits of human beings and of the mistakes we make if we assume what we are receiving is everything that's there. I feel that we need to hear more, see more, smell more, feel more.

James Dickey made a comment about your saying amazing things in your poems without raising your voice, as though you were "murmuring." But were you ever tempted to raise your voice?

No, I was not. I have always felt that a raised voice was a mistake, in the sixties or anytime. And in a way this is congruent with other parts of my life like the conscientious objection in World War II. I thought that, yes, I would like to go talk to Johnson, not stand outside hurling insults. Somehow communication implies hearing as well as saying; it implies listening; it implies understanding. And intellectual life in general implies a lot of intake, not just output. So that seems congruent with other parts of my life, to be murmuring. A murmur's enough.

Was there a way in which the sixties changed your life or your poems?

The sixties changed my life because it made poets very popular; poets traveled around the country. It enhanced the kind of popularity that had been growing. Economically, my life has greatly benefited from the popularity of writers and readings and workshops. The flourishing is manifested at workshops too. Many people come, having realized that writing is an access route to their deeper selves. I've felt and heard others talk about this fact, that many people who come to workshop sessions are like refugees from that world out there—the reverberating world.

Have poetry readings changed the landscape of contemporary poetry?

Yes, I think so. Recently I've come to realize that for many people the reading of their own poems to a group is a kind of breakthrough. It's a kind of achievement of participation in society. Apparently that's important. I didn't feel it myself, partly because readings didn't become popular until after I'd been writing for a long time. By then my pattern was already set, and I didn't feel elation about reading. I just felt that if they were ready to hear it, I was ready to read it. If they want to pay me, great. It means I'll travel well.

When you do give a reading do you feel a responsibility to read "Traveling through the Dark"?

No, I don't think I've read that poem for twenty years without it being requested. I don't feel I'm avoiding it, but it's not the kind of poem that especially interests me. Teachers tell me, and I believe them—I'm not trying to claim anything for it— that it's a good conversation starter in class. I'm glad for that.

But it isn't the kind of poem that I feel took me anywhere; I know how to write that kind of poem. I'm more interested in the ones I don't know how to write.

Have you shifted from technique-centered verse to voice-centered verse in the course of your career?

In the early fifties, I think it was, someone asked me to review a book about William Carlos Williams . . . and so I did. I read the work, thought about it, and I didn't think I was learning anything. I was already on that stream, I felt very much at home. Back home in Kansas in the thirties we would read *Spoon River Anthology*'s brief, sort of prosy vignettes of human beings; we delighted in them. It's a strange thing, the pessimism delighted us. I mean, "Petit, the Poet," and so on. Anne Rutledge and her stiff-arming of degenerate sons and daughters and so on . . . we liked that, and we thought that was *just;* it didn't depress us because it was so much fun to read. Well, as I say in one of my later poems about my mother and me, how we loved our town, how we chewed on its hard, tough rind and loved its flavor. There is feeling in some of the early, non-technical, non-metrical, non-rhymed language—language the way you hear it—that we liked.

Did you make a conscious decision to change the way you wrote?

I don't think any other way occurred to me than to write the best I could. Intellectually, I saw that one could try to be Swinburne, if one wanted to, and I did some things like that, but I always felt the satisfaction in writing was in entering the realm of communication with an equal use of the language of common people.

You do take up traditional forms occasionally, though not as often as, say, Philip Larkin, with whom you share an interest in both narrative and the use of the vernacular.

Yes, and I love his tough rind, his tough flavor. He seems quite bleak to most people, but I don't disagree with his point of view at all. Somehow I feel OK about it. The world is such a zestful place, even in its bleakness. Sometimes I've thought about what it would be like living in a country that said, "We're going to send you to Siberia." My feeling would be, "Well, great—Siberia, that's the place where, you know, all sorts of things happen." I suppose this is perversion, but I think I'm the kind of person who thrives on surmounting obstacles, the camp-in-the-snow type.

But many people were sent to Siberia to die or to live out their lives in exile.

Oh yes. There are extremes we cannot survive, extremes that crush the spirit, or almost do. That "almost" is important to me; we *can* continue to make distinctions wherever we are. Some concentration camps are better than others. I even got a whiff of that during World War II. Sometimes we danced in the barracks.

To go back to poetic form, you've mentioned the importance of prose for you as a writer. Perhaps prosaic qualities allow a toughness foreign to a Swinburnian style. How does a poetic form announce itself to you?

I think two ways. It is quite possible for me to shift gears and decide to write a form. It has never seemed to me a very difficult thing to do. But then I find myself, in my daily writing, drifting into an area where I feel the form hovering near what I've already naturally started to write. I'm quite capable of cultivating it. But for me the line break is something that's discovered as you move across the page; with any line you come to places where you get a gain or a bonus by breaking the sequence. I look for these bonuses. And if a bonus doesn't come along four or five stresses into the line, I create it. I mean I create the bonuses, by juggling the order of sentences or something like that. I don't try to *keep* from writing in a form. When you first said, "Well, you do write in forms," I thought that does sound like a violation of what I was saying about just talking across the table to someone. When I was a little kid, my parents would read me Robert Louis Stevenson, Kipling . . . formal things, mostly. So I was imbued with, penetrated with, those forms. They never felt foreign to me.

Do you have any feelings about the so-called new formalism? The view among some younger poets that free verse is a bit played out, or overplayed.

I do have a reaction to that. A poet like Richard Wilbur has been going along for years, steadily doing these elegant forms. I have felt the quality in what he has written, and often I feel totally committed to what he is doing. I don't feel thrown off a bit. But there are many poems that I find scattered around in magazines that just don't feel like *enough*. OK, they've got a rhyme, they've got a meter, but I don't feel the delight in it. It's got to have more. For whatever reason, I don't think I will ever feel the surge of delight in a poem just because it's in a form. And if I have the feeling it's in a form by the sacrifice of something else that I can almost glimpse, then I feel it is a disaster.

Do young poets you meet today have as good an understanding of craft and technique as poets did when you were starting to publish?

Maybe not, but they've got something else much more important. They believe it's possible to get the whole tide of their feelings and lives into the language that comes naturally to them, which is much more than the young poets had when I was starting to write. My own feeling is that the technical study of forms is not worthy of the time that writers are able to spend together in most workshops, considering the other things that we can do. A person can read a book if they want, and practice the forms on their own. It's like taking beginning Spanish in graduate school so that you can fill a language requirement. Sure, it's good to know Spanish, but you shouldn't have to do it in graduate school. It's a distraction, I feel, in a serious workshop to go back to describing what a sonnet is. That's not to say that you couldn't practice them; that's different. But to come to a writer's workshop in order to learn what a sonnet is seems a waste of money.

You're well known not only as a poet but also as a theoretician and teacher of the writing process. Have these activities had much effect on the way you write poetry?

Sometimes I think they have. And I don't feel good about that. My first impulse is to confess that I feel that I'm such a veteran of teaching writing that I can't get lost in a workshop; it's a natural, it's like breathing to me. Which is not to say that I don't feel nervous. I don't feel comfortable letting my theorizing in a writing workshop influence the free, onward feeling of my writing. I don't want to incorporate into the early stages of my writing process the laboriously achieved, step-by-step analysis that takes place sometimes in a workshop. I don't want that to have anything to do with my writing process. It makes me nervous. I may have sacrificed my instinctual self by teaching writing: I can't tell.

Do you usually do several versions of a poem?

Yes, I do. I write fast. I've been labeled by some as being a poet who writes too easily and therefore gets out a lot of junk. However, things that interest me I go back over. I do not feel committed to the idea that my work is perfect without my going back over it. Sometimes I go back over it many, many times. No matter how many times I go over it I don't ever feel that it's finished or that it has settled into what Yeats suggested: it clicks and therefore it's correct. I don't think that correctness or absolute rightness is in the realm of human possibility. So work is always revisable, as far as I'm concerned.

Despite the fact that you've traveled all over the world there isn't a great deal of exotica in your work. Why is that?

I remember when I was traveling in Pakistan someone asked, "Are you writing while you're traveling?" I said, "Yes." "Are you writing about Pakistan?" I was able to say yes, but I didn't want them to ask me more because at the time I was working on a poem about the patterns of cracks on the ceilings in hotel rooms in Pakistan. You know, there are cracks on the ceilings of hotel rooms in Cannon Beach, Oregon. So, I was at home. So much so that I wasn't a foreign traveler writing about an exotic place. I was a human being writing about his shelter for the night.

Has translating the works of others influenced your own work?

It doesn't feel like writing to me. It's like doing a puzzle. There is a kind of satisfaction, but it's a different feeling from writing my own work. A lot of the inducement, the motivation for writing is the discovery of the whole pattern. On the other hand, if you're running out of steam with your own writing, or you think you want to practice doing those adroit things that will redeem the subject matter shoveled onto the page, you can have those adventures working through the process of translation. But that's a long way from feeling the way you feel when you're writing your own things.

Do you have a sense of your own development as a poet?

I don't feel much urgency to analyze a line of development. It's foreign to my feeling about the process of writing. I remember reading that Auden said the problem for writers as they grow older is the fear of repeating oneself. I felt let down by this.

I believed Auden was exploring whatever came to him wherever it might lead, and then I find he is deliberately cultivating variety in order to either reach new readers or attain some kind of eminence as a poet. That doesn't interest me.

Do you have a sense of having accomplished what you set out to do?

No. Not at all. This may sound brutal, but I don't cherish the poems that are done. I cherish the poems that are coming. I'd sacrifice all the poems of the past for whatever is coming up. It's not a feeling of either satisfaction, or progress, or defending them. As far as I'm concerned, they're in the world to make a living for themselves if they can do it. I'm not going to do anything for them.

You put together a collection of your poems though.

Actually Harper and Row made the move about that. I think they decided, "Well, there are all these books, they're sort of in print, why not put them all together." There was an earlier book of mine they hadn't printed. That seemed fine to me.

Your most recent book is called You Must Revise Your Life. *Did you have in mind some difference between revising your life and Rilke's injunction to change?*

I intended the reverberation with Rilke. I thought, this is sort of fun. I didn't try to disguise it at all. I thought that readers who know Rilke will say, "Ah, yeah, here we go." I wanted to use the word "revise" because so many books about writing make it sound as though you create a good poem by tinkering with the poem you're working on. I think you create a good poem by revising your life . . . by living the kind of life that enables good poems to come about. It's much more productive, much more healthful, to feel you are embarked on a writing career in which the way you live your life has something to do with the kind of poems you write. I'm not suggesting being a kind of doomed poet—"I'll drink myself to death in order to write brilliant poems"—I don't believe in that at all! So I wanted to address all of that. And I wanted that resonance in the title: the echo of Rilke, and the strong assertion that writing good poems is more than revising the one you have in hand. Your life is a trajectory. A workshop may seem, to those who take part in it, a chance to revise the work they bring. I think it's a chance to see how your life can be changed . . . so that poem that began to come will be more satisfying, more fulfilling.

Is poetry a way "to bring strangers together," as you imply in your poem "Passwords: A Program of Poems"?

Passwords: A Program of Poems

> Might people stumble and wander
> for not knowing the right words,
> and get lost in their wandering?
>
> So—should you stand in the street
> answering all passwords
> day and night for any stranger?
>
> You couldn't do that.
> But sometimes your words
> might link especially to some other person.
>
> Here is a package,
> a program of passwords.
> It is to bring strangers together.

I remember writing that poem. I like to say things like that to see whether they'll fly. That poem didn't come out of conviction. It was more like an experiment: how do I feel about this? Well, I think language does bring us together. Fragile and misleading as it is, it's the best communication we've got, and poetry is language at its most intense and potentially fulfilling. Poems do bring people together. And not just the people who come to a workshop. But everybody—they are addicts of poetry without knowing it. Walking down the street, someone comes out of the church and says, "Oh, Bill, hello, been writing? How come people don't pay any attention to poetry these days?" When they've just been in church with hundreds of people reciting the Psalms in responsive readings, singing the songs, responding to the rhymes in the hymns. They are addicted to it. They're victims of it. And yet they come out and say, "How come people aren't interested in poetry?" It's because they've compartmentalized their minds. Maybe it's our fault that they feel that poems only appear in literary magazines. Poetry is everywhere. Here I am preaching about it. Oh yes, I think it brings people together. When they go to church and hear, "Though I speak with the tongues of men and of angels, and have not love," and so on, they're into poetry.

Interview with William Young, from *The Paris Review* 35 (winter 1993); "In Response to a Question," from *Poetry, Traveling through the Dark* (New York: Harper and Row, 1962), and *The Way It Is* (St. Paul: Graywolf Press, 1998); "Owls at the Shakespeare Festival," from *Mss* and *An Oregon Message* (New York: Harper and Row, 1987). "Passwords: A Program of Poems" was the title poem of a Sea Pen Press portfolio (Seattle: 1980) and of *Passwords* (New York: HarperPerennial, 1991).

Opportunities to Retrieve Paradise

Kit's Idea: The Good Dream

What if we all could hold in mind the same good dream. That is what a literary work accomplishes momentarily. Some day there may be a book so good that we hold the dream in mind permanently; we'll never escape it again.

There are infinite opportunities to retrieve paradise in words and in other art—to achieve it, though, by using the fragments around us in such a way as to hold paradise in *mind* no matter how lost it is in the emergencies of actual living.

The myth I hold is not that of the curse on the family, the guilt hovering forever as a result of a bad deed; but instead the vision of life haunted by some unerasable good deed: a life that can't lose for long, or at least forever. Not Oedipus doomed, but Aeneas bearing the unshruggable potential for later life—this is the pattern I note.

A Dream That Seems to Me Emblematic of
How to Write

I have bicycled up to a mountain town, and when I'm leaving— just at dusk—I can't tell which way to turn to go down; for a downslope may be just temporary, may be toward the mountain. When I go in a house to ask, I meet a person whose life surges into concert with mine in a conversation that reveals to us that pictures don't reveal meaning, and words don't, but drama does—the kind of drama we are experiencing together as we re- alize that events in our immediate association are leading for- ward through time in an enriching way, again, again, cumulatively, like notes of music. When I leave, turning right from the door, I know that I am doing the right thing, turning the right way, and that the person I have been with will come along if that is the right thing to do, but that in any event the leading I feel in my impulse is correct, a part of what is supposed to happen.

(This sure feeling is the feeling of doing art, when it comes just the way it wants to.)

Starting from an Idea in Nietzsche

We know that in *language* every word is a prejudice. All we *in*-clude implies millions of *ex*clusions. Even the pace has meaning. The language is the language of information *but* . . . (the game is not the game of information) order, proportion, significant subordination . . .

But enough—taking off in language now let me say

Not the news in our area but the *olds* is what continues its distinction here:

—the weeds along the creek
—the sky that has seen it all
—the main rise and fall of the land in its abiding gesture
—the air's constant, fluid accompaniment encouraging
  the lungs to enjoy and come back for more.

The Heaven of Experience

Art is the heaven of experience: out there in the intricacy of the object of art all human impulses are rewarded in terms of their inherent worth. Only alertness, justice, grace, readiness to accord valid and balanced and miraculously apt allegiances, etc., will bring rewards. Goodness pays and finds its own reward. No substitute for virtue is relevant.

As if by a miraculous return, literature is effective when it offers the materials of conviction and validation of real life: particulars, demonstration rather than soliciting.

Literature reinforces those tendencies which make for stability and confidence and effectiveness.

Events in literature turn into thoughts: with as many sides as there are dimensions in the reader's mind.

The Importance of the Trivial

We are surrounded, not by emblems, by paragons or villains, or fragments from Heaven and Hell, but by ready and adjustable potentials: nothing is special, everything is maybe.

This witness would note, confess, or assert, how small—how trivial—the elements which lead to a poem (or any work of art, or theory, or a truth) are. That is, the beginning impulse and perhaps the successive impulses too are often so colorless, so apparently random, so *homeless* and unaccountable, that most people would neglect them: they don't seem to amount to much. It is by lending faith and attention to these waifs of thought that we allow their meanings to develop, sometimes. And their mutual reinforcement is the composition of the poem, or the realization of any creative endeavor.

One further reflection it is only fair to make: in the perspective imposed here, all human perceptions, all experiences—no matter how grand or grandiose—accumulate from the concurrence of individually almost-insignificant elements; so the above assertion becomes, not a depreciation of art, but a realization about the provenance of human accomplishment.

All Meaning Grows from Relation

Theorists about literature have been far too timid. They thought they had reached a point at which only adjustments were needed. Far from it. All meaning grows from relation; the trying out of relations is the mind's function. Literature embodies that function and permits cumulative effects. To do anything is a comment on everything. Even literary failures push one into this creative realm. Non-literary people are *slugged* by complexity; a thinker, though, has millions of gears and alternative roads.

About Poetry

Present in the activity we often discuss—present in art—is something so great that we often turn away from it; we often settle for referring to minor things, like the topical relevance, or the cuteness or pace or finish of a poem. Or we may turn aside to regard the relation of the poem to some national or religious or social project of ours.

Beyond all that there is a certain thrum on important things that art sometimes achieves. It is as if a string is plucked that fastens to the stars, except that we know that size or distance is only a metaphor, only one way to hint at the quality meant here.

Of the ways to locate that thrum, the best I know is through a sudden confronting of *goodness,* but even that may be a metaphor: we all vibrate when we feel a certain resonance with what is.

"The Importance of the Trivial," quoted in part by Kim Stafford, *Early Morning* (St. Paul: Graywolf Press, 2002), 156.

Speaking of Writing . . .

Entering the Moment

We depend on two things—(1) the sense for words, the syllable-sense even, and the ability to grasp a pattern for saying; (2) the knack or luck or whatever for getting topics, themes, subject.

A poem succeeds, not by topic or form, but by a net forward effect.

Writing—the practice of entering the moment and looking around the way a traveler finds new country for the first time without knowing even its name.

Finding the Language

Speaking of writing, I usually welcome all kinds of impulses and ideas, not making an effort, during that first movement of en-counter, to restrict the cadence or pace or flow of the language. The feel of composition is more important than any rule or pre-scribed form. Swimmers after much practice can achieve a sense of catching hold of the water; the hand enters quickly and quickly adjusts to "the catch," the optimum angle and sweep for propulsion. I believe that the speaker and writer can cultivate that kind of readiness to accept and use the feel of the language.

Once anything is said or written, once the speaker or writer turns back to look at it, he may theorize in a number of ways about what he has done, in his freedom. And two such ways occur to me now.

One way focuses on syllables. Instead of assuming that the language has syllables with many sounds, only certain ones matched for rhyme or equivalent duration or emphasis, I assume that all syllables rhyme, sort of. That is, any syllable sounds more like any other syllable than it sounds like silence. This assumption confronts me with a whole torrent of immediate opportunities, in which the responsibility of the writer is not restricted to intermittent requirements of sound repetition or variation: the writer or speaker enters a constant, never-ending flow and variation of gloriously seething changes of sound. The responsibility is total—and the opportunities are also total. Once the writer accepts this total relation to the language, most discussions about meter and form (in regard to sound) become inadequate. The discussions may not be irrelevant, but they inevitably come as a series of distortions of the way writing *feels*. Like the swimmer, the practiced writer *finds* the material, an experience too rich for sequential explanation.

The other way of considering how it feels to write freely comes to me by way of a gradually sharpening awareness that the language—any language a speaker knows well—is really two languages at once. It is the language ordinarily identified by listless users, a temporarily fixed combination of words and denotations. But it is also stealthily and irresistibly a set of incipient meanings and influences which impose themselves on readers or listeners (or speakers or writers) by virtue of certain reinforcing patterns of sound which the language, as if by chance, has taken up into itself. That is, all syllables tend to slide by inherent quality toward certain meanings, either because of varying demands on the throat of utterance, or because of relations among clusters of syllables which have become loaded with associated meanings, and so on. I believe that this clustering of meanings operates everywhere in the language, but that its presence is easily evident to us only where its effect has become unusually marked. Words like slide, slick, slither, slime, sludge, etc., embody an *sl* sound which will steadily induce something of its potential meaning into any other words it gets itself into. Skid, ski, skate, scat, skull, etc., would immediately come to mind as another cluster. My belief is that the language is continuously under the influence of such currents or tendencies, and that alert or lucky speakers and writers ride such currents, with corresponding enhancements in their language. As a poet I am interested in living with such influences and benefiting from them. These influences are much more pervasive and subtle and helpful than any set of rules or verse forms could embody or anticipate.

The attitudes and beliefs expressed above make me, not an enemy of form or rule, but at least occasionally a roamer. And in writing I find that my practice initially is to roam forward through experience, finding the way as the process unfolds. This way with the language is interesting to me, and I believe such readiness is valid for living the language as we use it. Relying on forms or rules is always possible—is always one of the possible directions to take. But it is also possible that the everlasting process which led to discovery of forms and rules in the first place will continue to be worthy. Our experience with the language explores and validates and discovers. And that ever-new confrontation is essential for writing, even for effective writing in the strictest of forms.

So, respect for the achieved, along with readiness for a new achievement, is the attitude I would cultivate, and is in fact my prevalent feeling when I write.

The Form Is Found by Appetite

[In a poem] a thing shows up later because the feeling of relevance that gives you the signal as a reader was the same clue that brought the writer or talker back to this thing. The closure comes about, not because it's some trick, but because it's a natural thing. The form is found by appetite, not by calculation.

From a Box of Class Notes

The material itself sustains the values ordinarily said to sustain *it*.

Even the most distinctive ideas and principles have their basis in feelings, and hence can be subverted, inverted, enhanced and syncopated by imagination, so that their validity may be deliciously denied or perilously menaced, for shivers of experience.

One follows art; one finds myth—which reveals inner truth.

Literature is *not* real; and we must cease to value it for *realism*. It is the *departure from* actuality which distinguishes thinking, imagination, art, literature.

We drown in ugliness. Art helps teach us to swim.

About Making Literature

A person can tell about an event or feeling or scene, and in the telling find language that helps, that multiplies human response. A resonance of experience occurs. The language of information is being used, but the game (to hark back to Wittgenstein) is not the information game—it is something else. Potentials and residues of talk are awakened; a hearer or reader deliciously enters a shared existence in a world that feels large, outside the self, and alive. The world of literature and art.

"Finding the Language," from *Naked Poetry: Recent American Poetry in Open Forms*, ed. Stephen Berg and Robert Mezey (New York: Bobbs-Merrill, 1969); "[In a poem] a thing shows up . . . ," from "Diving for Dreams," interview with Charles Brashers and Sam Turner, *Writing* 2 (March 1979).

Some Suggestions from Experience

If you can get dumb enough you can write marvelous poems about things that are really close to you.

Where you live is not crucial, but how you *feel* about where you live is crucial.

The key to writing poetry may be a readiness. Relax, don't resist. Be a receiver.

Writing is effective in so far as it has verbal events in it, not the assertion of feelings.

We need to write poems that won't last forever.

Treat the world as if it really existed.

Try to listen to poems in neutral.

What starts a poem must validate itself. We need the sense of being in worthy company. Also the poem must earn its way. Every advance must be earned.

Competition is bad, I think. Even competition with yourself is bad.

Language is never the same. The same sentence repeated is not the same.

Inside the language we speak lies a secret language, an induced language: the language of bare syllables which have their own meaning.

An artist is a person who makes the decisions about the work the artist is doing. If you give that away it's not art.

Any chunk of carbon under pressure will turn into a diamond.

Poems are expendable, but the process is *not* expendable; it is lifelong.

What a person is shows up in what a person does.

We torture the limits of the language. Simplicity is more difficult than complexity.

What's on the page is more important than who is the writer.

Writing takes a lot of forgiveness, freedom, and welcoming. You should welcome the impulses that come to you. Don't try to stiff-arm your own feeble little thoughts. They are all you have.

Don't "strain the ratio"—don't ask the reader to do too much.

Be content to say the things we always wanted to say.

"Where you live . . . ," from *At the Field's End,* ed. Nicholas O'Connell (Seattle: Madrona, 1987); "Writing is effective . . . ," from "'People are Equal': An Interview with William Stafford," by Nancy Bunge, *Kansas Quarterly* 24, no. 4 (1993), and 25, no. 1 (1994); "Competition is bad . . ." and "Writing takes a lot of forgiveness . . . ," from "He Renders to God," interview with Mike Archbold, *101—Coast Magazine of the Arts* (autumn 1974); "An artist is a person . . . ," from "William Stafford on War and Peace," interview with Stephen Sander, *Spectrum* 2, no. 1 (spring 1978); "Poems are expendable . . . ," from "Fishing Your Life, Bonuses, and the Helicopter Arts: Interview with William Stafford," by Gala Muench, *Connections* (autumn 2001); "What a person is . . . ," from "An Interview with William Stafford," by Michael Fallon and Anthony McGurrin, *Maryland Poetry Review* (spring/summer 1988).

The Answers Are Inside
the Mountains

About Poetry

Is poetry a message? a performance? a stunt? a manifestation of a feeling, a thought, a glimpse? a prayer? Any of these?

Should poetry inspire? If not, is it all right if it does? Should it lead to action? Relieve from action? Not relate to action? If not, is it all right if it does?

Some poetry says, "Look at me." Some says, "I'm mad at the world." Some says, "Let's sing." Are these and other various calls for attention a mark of poetry? Are poets inviting others to engage for an interval in whatever topic the poem is on?

Assessing Writing

1) Is this topic significant? Yes.
2) Is the meaning clear? Yes.
3) Is the writer good? Yes.
4) Is the writing interesting? No.

Can this sequence be justified?

What Happens When You Say or Write a Word?

For me, the words go partway there, where things they say are. I think degrees of such awareness do exist, and stupid people may require stronger language than others do. The use of strong language is like the use of big, heavy, dusty equipment: you may need it some places, but trying to use it for work requiring clarity and accuracy and sustained progressions—that is sure to be frustrating.

Some questions should not be asked—or, at least, not answered; for an answer is an entry into a point of view or set of assumptions you may not really share. The answers are inside the mountains.

Are there words you should not hear? Are there sounds you should not hear? Are there people you should not meet? Are there thoughts you should not think?

II

On Workshops and
Poetry Classes

Meeting the Workshop

Preamble

Of all places, a workshop requires of me an absolute commitment to the text presented. How deep can I read? What profound realizations can come from this *evidence?* It is more than intention:—it is *revelation.*

Meeting the Workshop

Everyone will take part. The session depends on the people. What do you want from these sessions—*seriously?* From the texts before us will come enlightenment. The research paper of your life. It may be shattering.

I will hold before me the principle of immediate personal allegiance to the individual student. My central guide will be an *understanding* relation to the student. Hence, my job is to *listen,* receive signals of all kinds. My job is *not* to get excellence from the student (for "excellence" implies an already discovered model).

I can never legitimately praise or blame the "ability" of the student (for the *quality* of the student, the essence of the individual, is the ground of art). "If the fool would persist in his folly, he would become wise."

I will not test: to match an individual human being to a social expectation is a violation of the *creative* part of teaching. I will never sacrifice a student or the validity of human mutuality to society or my ambition. The curriculum will shrink to the size of the test. I think we should not lend our efforts to testing.

Conducting the Inner Light

In the class it takes a light touch. . . . What I want to propose is that we find what they're just about able to do and then we accompany them from that to what they're now able to do.

I'm a priest of the imagination, and when I go to class my job is conducting the inner light of those people to wherever it's going.

I think a little clue is, ideally, to have the class start from something *they* do, rather than something I do.

"In the class . . . ," from "A Priest of the Imagination," address given at National Council of Teachers of English conference, Louisville, Ky. (November 1992); "I'm a priest . . . ," from "'A Priest of the Imagination': A Conversation with David Elliott," *Friends Journal* (November 1991); "I think . . . ," from "William Stafford: A Conversation," interview with Richard Mathews, Dorothy Stafford, and Kathryn VanSpanckeren, *Tampa Review,* no. 2 (1989).

The Minuet

Sidling around Student Poems

My first impulse, when confronted with a student's writing, is to become steadfastly evasive until some signal from the student indicates a direction where the student is ready to go. I want to become the follower in this dance, partly because of some principles about what can be truly helpful in such an interchange, and partly because I have learned that the area between us is full of booby traps: the writer may have many kinds of predispositions, hang-ups, quirks, needs, bonuses. How the student comes toward me across that area is a crucially important beginning for whatever dancing there is going to be.

The first move is the student's move, not mine.

Of course, even handing me the writing is a move, and I am ready to give a slight twitch in return—slight, for a reason. And now I must try to formulate something about that reason. I assume that a writing—a poem, say—is sort of like an iceberg, with only a small part of its real self visible. If I am to be helpful, I need all the signals I can get, about the deeper drifts, the potentials, the alternatives actually ready to function for the main person involved—the student.

Not my life, my knowledge, my insight, but the student's whole life and potential are the main focus in our encounter. And I have to converge. Or so I see the process.

One Part of the Minuet

In some classes or under some circumstances we feel perfectly justified in considering what we read in terms of minimum paraphrases of what it says. We put doctrines or philosophies in alternative terms; we summarize; we trace derivations of basic ideas; we explore backgrounds and biographical relations. But in literature we somehow feel that such avenues of thought and discussion, no matter how often we do them or with whatever degree of immediate satisfaction, are misleading, are not sufficient, are not *literary*. What then is the distinction of the "literary" approach?

This issue stays puzzling. But some remarks suggest themselves. In literature, nothing is irrelevant. Our central concern is with total effect, and in experiencing that total effect, we work best when we make ourselves available to everything that happens in our encounter with the literature. Words that might be chance in history are *harnessed* in literature. What could be an example, used to make an isolated point in a brief or in a level explanation, is in literature either an effective part of the total experience, or a mistake. (Today many persons writing literature neglect something crucial when they launch chunks of assertion and analysis at their readers or hearers and carelessly or even perversely damage their effects by means of a voice or attitude that distracts the person who encounters the content.)

One aspect of literature that can be considered distinctly is that of *persona:* what is the effect of the being or the voice that is in the work? Is that voice the writer? Some chosen aspect of the writer? Some chosen vantage-character so set at an angle to the events as to maximize certain effects?

The Lifeboat

Saved by our lifeboat, *language.*

A Long Approach to a Poem—
The Way It Comes About . . .

It's four o'clock Friday afternoon. Students converge on the desk—the usual variety. One lags, holding the paper in her hand. Has the stealthy look of a creative writer.

The page is odd-size, no margins, no heading, messed up. Gold, though, is where you find it. How to meet this emergency? We look at what is here. It is little. It is something. It is real.

Once we've recognized it, we pause. Is there any more? The janitor's broom is coming down the hall. She goes one way, I another.

Is there a minuet for this?

"It's four o'clock . . ." A more developed version of this incident was used as the opening of "The Recognition of Discoveries," *College Composition and Communication*, 16, no. 5 (December 1965).

Goals

What Is It You Seek at a Writers' Workshop?

To publish? We can help; strangely, one of the easy things. To put into words what you know and feel? Inadequate reason: *find* what you know and feel. To teach and understand literature better? I think a workshop does give confidence and perspective. To discover something new, a new way to achieve something? Yes: writers are persons who write.

Evidence

What students write is not good or bad—it's evidence.

A Kind of Rhetoric

Have writing be not a program but an exploration. Once you have become convinced of something and you're trying to convince someone else, there's a kind of rhetoric that comes into the language that I immediately discount in my own life, and maybe I'm just trying to be careful not to give others any kind of a hint that I have a hidden program toward which I'm herding them. For most of us—and I would put myself in this group—the big issues are puzzling. They are not open and shut, and I do not feel confident myself of solutions about the really important issues of the day. I think they're complex, and most public discourse, I feel, is being done by persons who have insufficiently explored the complexity of the issues they're presenting. So that's on my mind when I'm doing this "active meditative" writing.

First Nothing

Art is first nothing, then something.

For Consideration in a Creative Writing Workshop

What elements in our experience do we identify with literary accomplishment? How do writers solve problems in working, when they have an idea but need to embody it? What do we recognize as meter and form in poetry? What actual procedures does the writer use? What guides do you have in judging your own work, or others' work—how are you led to make a new, a created product? Why write? What should one write? How about publishing?

Two Kinds of Writers

I want to understand where I am when I write; I want to get lost whenever I write a poem.

A Writing Class

Experience in writing is what the class offers, not "mastery," not "excellence," not even "good" pieces of writing. Assessment of the product is decidedly not the aim.

To let the individual student discover, or discover more fully, the help that using language can give in that individual student's life—that is the aim.

Participation in the group sessions is central to the class, for group discussion can help everyone experience that resonance that the act of writing can provide. The course is a part of one's life, and achievement on a test at the end is not the goal, nor will it measure one's accomplishment.

The goal is not the passing along of the teacher's knowledge, not the passing along of anyone's knowledge: the course sessions are meant to provide occasions for individual insights and encouragement.

There is a knack about writing; that knack apparently comes to the individual through performing the act of writing and the acts of considering writings. The aim is to induce a kind of jog through literature and its settings. It's a group project, the class; and if we can work it right the riches of the group will provide for us all.

Our Writing

Should we try for the perfect word? Should we try to write good pieces? No? Then what should we do? A bloodhound sets forth on a trail . . .

"What students write. . . ," from "A Priest of the Imagination," address given at National Council of Teachers of English conference, Louisville, Ky. (November 1992); "Have writing be not a program . . . ," from an interview with Barbara LaMorticella, KBOO Radio, Portland, Ore. (November 26, 1989); "Art is first nothing . . . ," from "Fishing Your Life, Bonuses, and the Helicopter Arts: Interview with William Stafford," by Gala Muench, *Connections* (autumn 2001).

An Allegiance to the
Most Tongue-Tied
A Discussion of Workshops with
Claire Cooperstein

From the interviewer's introduction: *On this languid August af-
ternoon* [at Haystack workshop, Cannon Beach, Oregon], *we
could hear the flute class and the class in steel drums rehearsing for
their farewell performances. We closed the door. I had read Stafford's es-
says on education in* You Must Revise Your Life, *a 1986 publication
of the University of Michigan Press. I pulled out my notes and began.*

*I notice that unlike most workshop leaders, you seldom "screen" partici-
pants by asking to see some poems in advance. Could you comment on
this? Is there a reason for your stance?*

Oh yes, I have a reason for that. Almost always, when I agree
to give a workshop, the person managing it says, "You know, of
course, you may decide on the participants—screen them, de-
termine a certain level, and so forth." I always reply, "I'll accept
them 'first come, first served,' or however you want to do it." I
do it this way for several reasons. For one thing, I don't trust the
screening process—it may exclude the writers I really do want to
meet.

There's another reason that occurs to me as I'm talking. My
job is accompanying an individual human being from where
they are to the next phase. That's how I see my role as a teacher.
If you are really going to be the kind of person in a group ses-
sion who listens, and is with them, and accompanies them to the
next increment, then you should not, at any point in the whole
process, be the kind of person who has demanded that they
reach a certain level before you will work with them. I'm willing

to be wherever they are. So, in an upcoming workshop, I'm going to teach the high school students, because the others wanted the more advanced writers. I said, "I'll take them—after all, I'm a teacher." No soul is going to be lost through screening.

Isn't the result of "no-screening" a mixed group such as you have here, that it will include some very verbal, very experienced people? Is it possible that the less experienced participants—through no fault of yours whatsoever—might begin to feel inadequate?

Well, I think this is a hazard in the group, but I think I can help them turn it into an asset in their lives. It's a challenge. With my help, they can see that they don't need to be afraid of those people. Those so-called confident people—they're quite vulnerable too, and we find that out together. I feel an allegiance to the mildest, the timidest, the most tongue-tied. And part of what we can do in a workshop is to be company for these people as we learn how to survive together.

A workshop of a few days, or even a few weeks, must be vastly different from a class that lasts a semester. In what ways do you adjust your unusual teaching methods to that condensed time frame?

For one thing, a writer's workshop is a short dash, rather than a long run. A few days, a week, or even two weeks is quite different from a ten- or fifteen-week term in a college, so you don't have time to do it the way I'd rather do it. The way I'd rather do it—the way it works best—is with time. You go in, you let it dawn on the students that something different is happening. But here at Haystack, I had to *tell* them it was different. I simply told them. So at the first meeting of a workshop, I usually have those considerations, usually talk about "Making Best Use of a Workshop" [see *You Must Revise Your Life* (Michigan, 1986)], even give them a "hand-out" on the subject.

I noticed you also had spent a great deal of time and thought on organizing the participants into three groups, and arranging opportunities for interaction between the groups.

That's right. We thought the safety valves would be that they could attend other people's sessions, could use this room for individual post-workshop conferences. All these things were designed to maximize participation, enabling the teacher to survive. Yet they're still nibbling away at me here. You heard what they were saying, that "we need to meet longer." [*Laughing.*] A group of students is like a bunch of piranha fish, you know—they'll eat you up. They could very easily take over the whole day and the whole night. So you need some respite in order to be able to do another workshop. But there's a nice ecology to workshops too. They get tired. Soon, they'd rather go to Bill's Bar than have a longer session, things like that. It works out.

So time becomes an important factor in planning a workshop?

Oh yes. Essentially the difference between teaching a course in college for a term and teaching a one-week workshop—there are several differences—but an important one is the matter of time. You've got to engage fast . . . no time to sneak up on it. The other thing is that people in a workshop are a different society from those in a college class.

That's one of the things I wanted to ask you about. Do you enjoy interacting with the average workshop participant—the more mature student with more life experience?

The more mature they are, the more at home I am. I do feel easier with them. After all, at my age, that's part of it. But also, the people in workshops seem more sensitive, easier to reason with somehow. Even the timid ones who are quick to sense whether you are threatening or domineering, very soon find out I'm not. So I feel happy about that—since I really am not. But I have been to workshops in which older people, even tough people, have been utterly crushed. In a way they're more vulnerable because their days are more precious now, the marginal value of a day is greater than a college student's—*their* days can be thrown away—after all, ahead are millions of them. But for a person in a workshop . . . they bank a lot on this time. They've used their vacation time to come, and they've brought something that has become precious to them, part of their lives—this writing. They're already committed to writing; often college students are just taking it as one of the courses.

". . . It sounds like fun and it doesn't sound like too much homework."

Right. So at a writer's conference, the pace is different, and people are different. You are experiencing what seems to me to be a fairly typical writer's conference here. Even the things that seem to emerge to my surprise, are not to my surprise. For instance, they want to meet longer—that happens in other workshops, other places. In general, this is typical. It's the other, the college teaching, that takes a different kind of finesse—at least to do my kind of teaching.

Is there a correlation between "The Box" you described as part of your college teaching (a box placed in the library's reserve shelf, into which students were encouraged to place poems and essays) and "The Wall" you introduced in this workshop? (Stafford had encouraged participants to post poems, essays, comments on one long wall. By the time we met for our interview, the wall was full, with poems posted top to bottom, end to end.)

Yes, I feel there is. This is a faster way to do it. And less cumbersome. It's our own wall, in our own room. See how it's flourishing . . .

It certainly is! And you started it all with your little poem. (The morning after announcing the purpose of The Wall, Stafford had posted one of his "before-breakfast" poems—a few lines, hand-written and signed.)

One little poem, that's all it took. People saw that it's possible to put their poems up, get a little feed-back. No hazard to it. It is like The Box—in some ways it's better than The Box. At the college, it wasn't possible to use a wall. There was never a classroom that was solely yours. I think I prefer it this way.

You do? As I recall, at the college you encouraged the students to go through The Box often, write comments on each other's poems—and they did. Here it's such a public place. Even though you suggested that people might want to write comments on the poems, I notice that no one has.

No they haven't, perhaps because it *is* a public place. But I've heard them talking about the poems to each other. And that's what's crucial—this opportunity for communication.

In your essay on education ["A Priest of the Imagination"] *in* You Must Revise Your Life, *you explain why you feel it important for a teacher to withhold praise as well as blame. Yet, at least in this workshop, I noticed the group often praised. I was surprised that I never heard you cut it off. Can you tell my why? Isn't it almost the same when a workshop member says, "I really like your poem!"*

Well, you'll notice I always say, "This is a workshop—you've got to tell us why you like it." And that's my move. Then, too, I feel there's a difference, in both college class and workshop. If the teacher—workshop leader or whatever—alters the group's judgment (with either praise or blame), that skews the discussion. The teacher has a lot of leverage—you don't have to claim it, you don't have to prove it, they just give it to you—that's why they came. So if you enter in, alter the group's judgment, it's harder for the dynamics of the group to work.

So you, as the teacher, withhold judgment—but don't interfere with the judgment of others?

Yes. It's all right for society to make a judgment—after all, language is social, and I think that's one of the lessons to be learned. It's something that works on the group, and not on the critic.

Do you occasionally come across students who cannot accept your non-judgmental, non-directive methods?

Yes. In both college classes and workshops like this one, there are people who have great difficulty accepting the stance I take toward the writing process. College students will come around and say, "Please—you've got to tell me, put a grade on this, tell me what you think of it."

And in workshops like this?

You sometimes find people who also insist, "I want to know what I'm doing right and what I'm doing wrong—a specific critique, so I can fix the poem . . ."

And this, of course, is something you don't do?

Right. And sometimes I feel vulnerable about this. Why am I so reluctant to do it? It would certainly be possible for me to take a poem and say, "This is what you ought to do with it—this and this and this." I could do that, but there are several reasons not to. For one thing, I'm not absolutely sure. Though by now I've got quite a bit of confidence in what I do, still, there's this natural diffidence. But also I think I would be diverting them from what seems to me the primary purpose of a writer's conference: to learn to be self-critical, to become aware, through interaction with other people, that language is social. If I did this, they might think that language is something you could learn— chop it up and play it like checkers. But it really is something even more complex than, say, chess, or any game you can think of. I would not want to consolidate these feelings—that there are certain limited moves we can make to revise poems toward publication. I think that what we can learn here is much richer than that. We can learn to shape and form our poems in relation to ourselves, so that they become satisfying to us at the same time that they become invaluable to some other readers.

From your previous essays on education, I'm under the impression that you consider "craft" one of the less important things to be taught. Do you think it needs to be taught at all?

I think that it will be acquired in the course of your writing and in your interchanges with others. And it's better to be acquired as you feel the need for it, than in chunks: "This is what I must learn," and so forth. But even things like form—it doesn't seem worthy of a grown-up's time to be counting syllables. It's like going to graduate school to learn Beginning French.

Can I play devil's advocate for a moment?

Yes, of course.

As you know, I recently received an M.F.A. in Writing from Vermont College, an innovative, low-residency program. It involved a great deal of marking up directly on the poem, always accompanied by a gentle letter of explanation, saying things like "Perhaps you might like to consider this." And I found this very specific, directive approach quite helpful. I agree with you that the essence of poetry is the realization of the inner self, but I'm not sure you can teach that. It seems to me the only thing you can teach are the appropriate techniques.

[*Laughing.*] You *are* a good devil—by which I mean a bad devil! I think I glimpse clearly what you're saying. You can teach those things, you can't teach the other, why not teach the things you *can* teach? Well, first I want to make a distinction between college students and workshop students. College students are so much in the habit of being molded by their teachers that it is much more important to lean back, let them experience the loss of the safety net, let them learn to walk the tightrope by themselves. While in a workshop, I can come at least part way toward your devilish proposition, because these people are more mature, and have built into them the realization of what it means for human beings to interact. With college students, it's more important that I do *not* perpetuate the hand-on-the-head feeling. But in a workshop, I can go a lot farther toward making intrusive, direct suggestions. And I often do in individual conferences.

And in the group meetings?

In the group meetings, it's different. There are a number of reasons you want to get the group to interact. For one thing, at a writer's conference you are almost certain to have a cadre of people who are quite knowledgeable; published writers (or if not yet published, could be published), people full of insights, wisdom. It behooves me to get them on my side. If I don't lean back enough to get them to take part, we'll all be deprived of this richness. I've discussed this with other workshop leaders. Some who seem sympathetic will say, "Yes, Bill, I share your ideas. I always encourage the group to enter in, and I don't come in till the end." Well, of course, that spoils it all—if you come in at the end!

How do you handle the problem?

I'm going to confess to something really audacious. The group has been talking. The writer has got some, what seems to me, terrible advice from the group. We're ready to go on to the next poem, and the right things haven't been said yet. Well, I don't say them, I just go on anyway. Because if I entered in then, saying, "This is the way it ought to be," I'd spoil all the other group engagements. The whole workshop would turn into a charade.

Yet I remember hearing you say, very gently, and in a very devious way, things that you seemed to think needed saying.

Yes, of course. But this is what's crucial: the receptivity or lack of receptivity of the student. You need to say it deviously, and quietly, and insinuate it rather than steamroll it. It's important how they feel. They need to have a mind-set and an emotion-set that enables them to take what comes from outside, and have it be productive. I've gone to conferences and listened in on workshop leaders who were quick, intelligent, excellent teachers— and they just killed the class. They got no conversation out of the group whatsoever, just because they immediately came forward with something strong. The student heard it, but couldn't accept it. What I do is try to make them think, "Well, that's kind of my own idea too . . ."

One final question. Realistically, what do you think a dedicated participant can expect to gain from a workshop such as this?

Realistically, and really what happens is—a workshop can easily have, and does have a profound effect on many people who participate, as you have probably witnessed right here this week. People can't believe how much difference it makes to them to discover others who share this urgency that they haven't been able to give a name to, this feeling that there might be something in writing for them. And they discover that if they enter into this process with words in a sustained way, in an encouraging atmosphere, they will discover that parts of their lives that were only faintly realized suddenly are more fully realized. Those who think they come just to learn how to write something they can sell to a magazine far underestimate what they get from a workshop.

Those writers who have immersed themselves in poetry and literature for several years—as I noticed many of those in your group at Haystack have—what do you think they get from a workshop?

It varies with the person. Many who have been writing for years and who have experienced workshops before, I've had in my workshops before. So I can't say this is the first time they get a taste of this thing I'm claiming. But I think all of us need confirmation of what's happened, we need renewal. It's a very warm community feeling that almost always evolves in a workshop that's conducted the way this one has been, in which those in the group begin to like each other, one might almost say love each other. They suddenly realize that we're on a voyage, in which having the presence of others with more experience is a great bonus. And even those who have written for years may have slipped into—it's quite easy to slip into it—treating writing as a commercial venture, something to feed your ambition. The presence of a large number of people who are using writing for fuller realization of the self will redeem them from the ego building, the ambition simply to become famous.

What you seem to be saying is that in workshops such as this one, both the novice and the experienced can learn something very special, something besides learning how to write.

Exactly. Recently I met a former student who told me, "It's all too overwhelming what happens. All sorts of things sweep in upon you. You're drowned in opportunities for rescuing and making something of your life. It's overwhelming—that's why I'm here again."

Interview with Claire Cooperstein, from *Poets and Writers Magazine* (March/April 1990).

A Memory Map Exercise

Early in 1992 William Stafford and Stephen Dunning were putting finishing touches to their National Council of Teachers of English writing book, Getting the Knack. *At the end of January William Stafford spent one of his morning writing sessions on a memory exercise planned for the book. This exercise, described in full on pages 95–106 of* Getting the Knack, *involves the recovery of childhood memories, in several steps, starting with literal memory items, then moving to imagination items, on to a closer focus on individual items, and finally to poem drafts. The resulting poem, "Third Street," was published in the volume, but not the memory notes, which are given here.*

Step One: Imagine being back in your home at the age of five or six.

Step Two: Draw a floor plan of your room in that house.

Step Three: Memories. Remember things from that room, and place them on the plan.

a) Copies of "The American Boy" and library books by my bed. *Two Little Savages:* E. T. Seton.
b) I don't have any secret things. (But my slingshot hangs on the bedpost.)
c) My dog Buster sleeps beside the bed.
d) We don't hang anything on the wall. (Quaker influence.)
e) Our games are outside—jump rope, hopscotch on sidewalk.
f) Peg has dolls. No soldiers, stamps, cards in our house.
g) My usual dress is bib overalls, blue shirt, elkhide shoes.

Step Two   Memory Map!

our 3rd street house

Peg's bed   dresser

          door   Hall

rug   Living Room
          Fire
          Place

my bed

closet   door

          Porch

          steps

3rd St.

Vinegar
factory

h) My knife is in my overalls pocket.

i) No money. Some string. My survival kit—matches, fish hooks.

j) The rug is the best furniture—Buster there.

k) No pictures, except in Wells's *Outline of History.*

l) No bed light, heater, clock. My hammer and saw in the basement.

m) Cousin Ed gave me a kazoo (in overalls pocket).

Step Three: Imagination. Add further items to the plan.

n) Down the street I can see the vinegar factory. Beyond, I know, is the Santa Fe track, then the Arkansas River.

o) No scary place in my room—Buster is there.

p) When I read *Two Little Savages* Buster and I are lost—but brave—in the wilderness.

q) I'd always show off Buster if I could.

r) I'm never punished, but I can imagine being alone.

s) Buster and I talk. He tells me about Alaska.

Step Four: Write comments on selected items.

b) and h) My father reminds me that—like the cave men in *The Outline of History*—I could survive anywhere with my own efforts, especially if I always have my knife and my slingshot. And Buster could help too.

*d) and f) More and more I realize that our family is different—we don't hurt people (no soldiers); we live simply (no exploiting of others); we don't punish anyone—children are free and encouraged.

g) But we do make music, a kazoo and singing—and on our Victrola we have Caruso and Madame Shuman Heink.

*n) The vinegar factory burned one night. My father held me in his arms as we watched. I shivered, and he asked "Are you cold?"

o) Our room is always safe. I can hear trains. I can

imagine the gray water of the river. The world goes on out forever. I could go there.

*r) My mother and father encourage me—I can explore, hike anywhere, read anything, choose my friends. Oppression or punishment I have to read about or imagine.

s) These imaginary adventures I talk over with Buster.

f) Why have I left out Peg? She is my friend, and her friends visit and talk. But they don't hike to the river, or have slingshots or knives.

Step Five: Put asterisks by the most significant items, and comment on them.

Items d) and f) Like a clean, airy tent the smell of the vinegar factory works arched over our house, and that sharp, clear feeling it gave surrounded our lives. Other kids' fathers and mothers might punish and swear; and we heard that some drank and brawled. Jean's parents, across wide Third Street, were like that. Why should anyone be other than curious and kind and free? Peg and I inhaled that vinegar, proofed against all that surrounded our neighborhood. I can't remember any temptation to drink, smoke, swear. Were those temptations? We smelled freedom that was clean.

Item n) Late one night my father waked me to see the fire—great streamers of flame from the vinegar works. It was cold on our porch and I shivered—safe but watching the world burn down. I told my father I was just cold, but really I was afraid.

Item f) Peg followed her life. I'm with her in our room, and we talk about friends. She admires my adventures and shivers about my plunge in the river, the ice all around. She loves Buster, but Buster comes to my side.

Step Six: Write a poem draft.

Third Street

Dying right there in my room, seven years old
and I'm dying. "Dip-therea," we call it, and my throat
won't open, the doctor's long needle stabbing my back,
Buster my dog whining, Peggy holding
her doll and crying. Shadows lengthen and reach
on the wall. They jump. They are watching me die.
And the doctor shaking his head at my mother.

Now in the strange room of my head the shadow
escapes and floats away, leaving our street,
the vinegar factory; rolling past the twin tracks
and fluttery lights; gone into the sky, diminishing the
    river.
How sad that my dog on his little rug will sleep
alone, that my sister's doll will stare button eyes
all night at my empty bed.

If only my father could hold me forever, and the world
stay still—my little blue shirt, my elkhide shoes
waiting for Buster and me to explore Alaska
and all those ranges. . . . I see our clean walls, and the
    sparrow
I killed with my slingshot (how it held out its wings and
    fell
trembling into the dust). I will live. The doctor's
black bag will save me. His long needle will stab
into my back, and Buster will howl.

My father's eyes—I see them yearn me toward him
and bring me drifting and weak to my bed in the room.
Years later when my son dies that look
will return and something will break in the sky that was
    welded
at home and forged by a thousand pledges of truth.
Third Street, I have you here, and my throat will open.

Steps Seven and Eight: Write a final version; copy the poem into
your notebook.

Reflections on Doing Memory Writing, and on "Third Street"

All over again I am reminded of the surge of freedom there is in letting my writing find its own way, letting it get "creative."

In daily life my ears and eyes are subjected to language serving the programs and egos of intentional people—selling, getting elected, currying favor, stalking my pocketbook or soul. I get used to that, but it is suffocating.

There is an escape, though—a breath of oxygen. It comes with a great, stringent surge when language realizes itself, leaning into a transformation—into art, into poetry. The speaker or writer surrenders to what begins to *happen* in language, what it discovers when it encounters—not a prepared or accustomed stand or position—, but a possibility, an emerging entity never existing before. There is a single, pursuing loyalty that gives itself to the line of development growing from experience as it comes along.

And that line is always new, a surprise. Maybe a poem.

Other portions of this exercise appeared in *Getting the Knack,* ed. Stephen Dunning and William Stafford (Urbana, Ill.: NCTE, 1992). The final version of "Third Street" appeared there, as well as in *Poetry* and *The Way It Is* (St. Paul: Graywolf Press, 1998).

Workshop Insights

1

When others talk of their new, encouraging way to approach writing, they often give me some disquiet—are we really convergent on that? Can I account for my disquiet?

Those others continue to aim for "good" writing. What does that mean? Do I clearly hold that the writing should be, rather, *valid* writing? Something that drapes exactly on some kind of undisguised inner reality? My impulse is to say that the product should not be "improved" but be somehow more translucent, be a product of the right way to *act*. More on this.

The "quality" of writing cannot be assessed by an inventory of what is there and what is well managed. What *isn't* there? What achievement here has come from suppressing *another* kind? What ultimately sacramental value is linked to this piece? Is this act of writing *healthful*? For the writer? For the reader? For the universe? More on this.

The relation of teacher and student—does one's approach foster an attitude of dominance? Is the from-me-to-you process conducive to a desirable joint effort? Is one person prevalently to be maintained as source and the other as receiver? What effect on source? On receiver? More on this.

A few odd reflections. Certain tones or attitudes create their own universes of discourse. One can be instructional, or analytical, or entertaining, or spectacular, and so on. It might happen that only irony is a valid stance; for only the attitude of turning over the drawing of conclusions by the "student" is compatible with a long-term intellectual achievement. Flashes of brilliance may blind us; exciting performance may weaken rather than enhance the mutual forwarding of realizations. You shouldn't ever impress.

2

Poets are after *other* communication. They often have even a mystical impulse, extra-sensory impulses . . .

Things you feel strongly about, they recur, no matter what you are writing or *intending*.

Maybe you could write a poem as it comes, with connections between the parts, and then erase the connections so as to induce a leaping or flying sensation on the part of the reader or hearer. Leaps in syntax could be an *advantage*.

A poet might even like to be misunderstood—for misunderstanding is richer and more varied than understanding.

Where the poem comes from is of more interest than what the poem does.

When you dry up while writing, that is the end.

The end should relate to all before it.

Victor Hugo said, "Even when the bird is walking we know that it has wings."

3

The grammar of a sentence is analyzable in structure, but the *sound* and *meaning* of a sentence are dependent on elements more numerous and complex than is the grammatical structure.

4

Experiences that particularly strike you.

It's important to *me*, if not to my poem.

Too much alliteration? How much is enough?

Spacing is punctuation—sometimes.

How do you *choose* words?

Give something expected; give something unexpected.

A poem gives something new.

5

The stance of the writer or speaker of a poem is a pervasive influence on the poem's effect; yet we often neglect to consider that pervasive influence. Some stances:

a) I am telling you something I think you don't know.
b) I am telling you something you already know, but are ready to hear rehearsed.
c) The material is telling you something that you wonder if I also know.
d) I am pretending to tell you something but we both know the real direction of the poem is elsewhere.
e) The poem is suggesting something.
f) The poem is suggesting something, but the overt statement is something else (irony?).
g) "I" address "you" inside the poem, describing something we are both aware of, but I am really addressing the reader or hearer of this poem ("We were standing by a lake. You looked at me and said . . ." etc.).

6

Upset people say poetic things.

Some people are so much in favor of free speech that they don't give you a chance to talk.

Getting a kinetic start, getting a pulse in the language, setting the lines. Prose is with punctuation; poetry is with bonuses.

Ghosts in a poem. Rifle quiet.

A dialectic of composition, scene—panorama—scene.

Risk misunderstanding to gain intensity.

Press the reader's hands onto the roughness of experience.

Lectures often have this contradiction: you know enough to appreciate what I say—but you are so ignorant that I must tell you elementary things.

If your thoughts are clichés, your language should be clichés.

Have good dreams, know when a dream is right, read good material, see useful things, overhear relevant things, bring in helpful fragments, honor your experiences.

7

Student activity should be *for the student;* teacher-checking is itself potentially discouraging.

Assessing may be necessary and good. But *learning* requires a masking of assessment.

Journals are private; derivatives from the journal could be public.

Each student has a periphery of learning. Where that periphery is can be found by the student, not the teacher.

8

In your writing do you try to tell people things they already know, or things they don't know? This time, tell something that you are the world expert on—something that only you know. Never express anything you assume the reader already knows—inform the reader. No fair saying commonly accepted things—there must be at least a twist on what you say.

Is euphemism bad?—dishonest? Is bluntness honest? Using some character or persona that you imagine for the purpose, write with either evasiveness or bluntness, but in each instance make your reader somehow aware that the speaker is consistently being either evasive or blunt—make the manner of speech be evidence for your reader's perception of a meaning behind what is actually said.

9

Common faults: You leave the scaffolding. You stiffly locate a stance and don't move from the expositional mode, the "I am telling you" tone. Excess of soliciting over *demonstration*. Not enough verbal events and felicities.

The third paragraph of section 1 ("The 'quality' of writing . . .") first appeared in Kim Stafford, *Early Morning* (St. Paul: Graywolf Press, 2002), 161.

The Classroom Contract

This fall I undertook a course in a language foreign to many students: "Edited Written English." My intention was to accept any slanders and slights against my topic, but to teach it, facing it as one of the ways to communicate—and a way that had many accompanying advantages for any practitioner.

For reasons fairly honorable this course had only qualified success, one reason being the unexpected and unstoppable creativity of the students. When business letters began to show up with flourishes of irony in them, I knew I had problems. But generally we pursued our intention, and I want to use our experiences in this course as a reference point, a way to keep track of some ideas meant to relate directly to our jobs and to our lives.

Maybe it would not surprise you (though as I recall the topic surfaced unsolicited in an early class session) that the students raised the issue of honesty in relation to our subject: "When you become more adept in wielding language, can you be as honest as you were before?" We didn't belabor this issue in class, but it stuck in my mind, and I carry it still. "When you become more adept in wielding language, can you be as honest as you were before?"

Let me drop back for a minute and put a frame around this experience that underlies my report. Years ago when I was starting to teach there was one colleague often envied by others. She heroically taught, held to standards, was the kind of composition teacher who wrote more on the paper than the student had written. At a party once I found the courage to confide in her, "Composition class is so hard—I can't keep up. It's a great burden. As you go on, does it get any easier?"

And she said—I can remember how my heart sank at this—

"It gets harder and harder." She was saying, partly, that she found herself more and more aware of responsibility, more and more burdened by how she thought she had to do her job. And I saw the years stretching ahead of me, down, down, into the late smothered-by-papers hours. I resolved then to try for something happier. I want to witness for a way to accomplish our work without that self-defeating submergence into the routine. I want to explain, justify, take a stand.

I'm scared all over again as I say this. It's like setting up a hurdle for myself, and then trying to make it. I want to help set us all free. I suppose that's one reason we meet at times like this. How can we do it? Well, after that chilling conversation, for many years I could ask myself each fall: "Have I read and studied enough to be a good teacher?" And I had an answer that kept me reassured for years: "No. I have not read and studied enough. I am learning." But one year a frightening thing happened. I asked myself the question, and my answer had to be: "Yes, I have read and studied enough." But a further question naturally came: "Am I now a good teacher?" And the answer was: "No." This time, I didn't know where to turn next.

Today I want to do my best to speak about where to turn next. I want to establish a basis for all the local tricks. I want to establish the implied contract under which I will always teach. This implied contract is something that has grown, like coral, silently while experience accumulated. The local tricks are not really tricks, I believe, when done in the light of the "contract." Actually, it may be that the "tricks" are just incidental results of pursuing a steady intention. This is what I hope. And I want to circle around this intention for awhile, for I found it essential, like a compass, like a map, through this wilderness we plunge into Monday mornings.

To find this contract in words, this implied classroom contract, I must ramble a little bit now. Above my classroom door (in invisible paint of course) it says: "Take hope, all ye who enter here." My job as a teacher requires of me immediate allegiance to individual students who come through the door. I know that I have other jobs—to survive, for instance, to be a citizen. But as teacher, my first leaning is simple in its first response: "Who's there? Where to from here? How can I help?"

The overwhelming consideration is: this student.

Over the years, this stance has induced a whole set of assumptions about my relation to students. Some of these assumptions can hardly surface in certain situations, and I'm ready to adapt. But it is surprising how many of these assumptions can work, even in apparently frustrating systems. I want to mention some of those assumptions.

(I have taught high school. I have taught in big university systems where I was to be the front line and flunk out a third or a half of the students who were having trouble. This was back when we had waves of students. And I have visited many kinds of schools. I say this sort of defensively at the beginning, because I know some of these assumptions are going to sound idealistic or as if they would work only in certain situations. I'm always ready to adjust in order to survive, I must confess. This is what I'd like. I've just made a list of policies, under the classroom contract that I'm trying to live by.)

Attendance: Any person registered for the class has a right to attend all regularly scheduled meetings.

Talking: Any person in the class has a claim to be heard in discussions. No one will be forced to speak. It is understood that some like to speak when they want to speak, and to be silent when they want to be silent.

(I want to mention a very recent incident. A class, not too large for me to keep track of. I'm not an expert at this, but this was about twenty-three students or so. I began to notice a great discrepancy between the writing of one student, a very quiet student, and the contributions of this student in discussion. Not a word in class. And then, suddenly, these written responses that galvanized me. This ought to be part of our class. This was the only person in class that I spoke to, and then I did it in a sly way, toward the end. When she happened to spill some books or something and was a little late leaving the classroom, I pounced and said, "Didn't you volunteer to start the discussion one of these times?" This was a maneuver: each time I would say, "Who'll start the discussion so the teacher won't talk too much?" I could always get someone. And she was startled. She said, "No. I didn't volunteer." I acted as if I thought she had. I said, "Oh, all right." And then she said, "But I will." This student for me is like a test case. She didn't quite have the nerve to do it. But she was looking for an excuse to do it. And when I asked her, OK, she did. Well, . . .)

Writing: Any person in the class has a claim to participate in the frequent occasions for writing in class. No one will be forced to write. And no one will be "corrected," though as in talking any request for particular reactions will be honored.

Ratings, rankings, grades, records, etc.: The course is designated as "credit, no-record"; any person wanting a grade can follow procedure set by the Registrar's office. Grades given will be based on quality—no special projects. The instructor will go into a trance at the end of the course and provide a mark, if requested to do so.

"Difficulty," etc.: The course is easy, no hazards. Minimum involvement can be very light. At an extreme of involvement, the course could be a career.

Hovering over the sessions will be a hope, a hope for circumstances to enable the building of a feeling for our course. I have come to a kind of still-hunter's set of superstitions about capturing this right feeling. This is where it goes into something strange. It can't be a list. There's some kind of feeling about it. I no longer stride into class, that important first time, with the outline in my hand and with a clear set of instructions as we go along. Instead, I am wavery; I am roving the room, the weather, the expressions for guidance. I want to become a responder, a listener—an immediate learner. Things change as sessions go along. I make notes of what students say.

(A couple of years ago I was teaching a short term at the University of Cincinnati, and this had become so automatic for me that I was sitting there, and some student said something, and I immediately distracted myself from what was going on and began to write. And a student said, "What are you doing?" I said, "Well, I'm writing down what so-and-so just said so I can think about it later." And this person said, "You're the first teacher I ever saw that made notes on what the students said." Well. I not only do that, but I use what they say.)

And one way to tag this classroom still-hunt I'm describing is to confess that my ideal for a listener these days or a reader-participant as the student's paper passes under the scansion of writer and teacher, is this: the listener-reader has a wonderful rubber face. It registers not praise or blame, but a million hopes, anticipations, hesitations, despairs, triumphs, doubts, rages . . . Envy. Recognition. Sympathy.

For it has come to me that our debates about praise or blame, our attempts to load on comments, or to withhold them, these miss the life of composition. It has come to me recently that all my worry when I asked this veteran teacher about how it is, and she says it gets harder and harder, I was assuming, as I guess most of us assume, that our job is some kind of assessment. I don't think that's right any more. It's not praise or blame. It's not how many comments. But something like: where is that flicker of individual meaning? Am I perceiving recurrent patterns? Can I glimpse the tentativeness of a student's thought and wording? Is there a place in this paper where the writer is at the point of confirming or abandoning a crucial impulse? Where is the periphery of realization for this student in this paper? (I don't have any special claim for my phrasing, but I recur to this because to me it's a way to keep track of what I'm trying to do. That periphery of realization: as a teacher, where that is, is not my job. Being where it is, is my job. And I am listening for that.)

If I can see that periphery of realization for this individual student, or if I can guess it, or even—maybe—if I can *invent* it, I can respond meaningfully without trampling all that individual area the student rightly comes to cherish as a *self* not to be owned by others. (I've learned just this term that by the end of a course now I can face the world with each student. It came to me as a result of trying many things.)

Now the kind of composition I'm assuming here, and the kind of conversation, comes from a certain feeling of community in the room. The kind I'm looking for—and this is as near as I've come to a brief statement of the classroom contract—is: the feeling that permits us to say the things we know, to say them at the right time, with a place then for what we don't know, and an acceptance of not knowing, and a readiness to be surprised only by good surprise—the kind that finds meaning. In a room of people we help each other come to things we know. The contract unspoken among us will enable us to say and to hear. We seek that kind of contract.

I don't work for the administration. I work for each student. First things first. A student who writes has said something. Are you going to pay attention? To me, even the most cursory reading that is quick is in some sense allowable if it's timely. I can imagine a student handing in a paper and saying, "Did you hear me?" And I can imagine my answer always can be, "Yeah, I heard you." And the implied resultant is—What's next?

After class a student was talking to me about a paper on the desk between us, and I asked, "When you wrote this paper, were you telling your reader something they already knew, or something they didn't know?" This seemed a fairly harmless question to me. But there was a long pause. And then a strange smile came on that student's alive face. She had been going through a charade in school, she confessed. It hadn't occurred to her to make her goal the telling of something *to a teacher.* She told me—she was an excellent student—she thought she had to *tell it back.* We agreed that I'd try to keep from cluttering up her life, if she'd try to keep from cluttering up mine. And she'd tell me things I didn't know.

The paper she wrote at the end of this course was "Letter from an Editor." She said one of the initial and most persistently haunting questions that I posed was defining what edited writing should be. I let the silence go longer and longer, partly so I could think more and more. Partly just because it's a good idea. Then the longer I let it go, the harder I thought it was to answer, at least briefly. The student said, "I concluded that the fundamental qualification is that the writing be reviewed and revised until all the language usage, whether conventional or improvised, is intended." This conversation I had with this student taught me something I didn't know. It led to a new kind of classroom assignment, a paper on things nobody else in this class knows. I got all sorts of things.

From "Teaching Edited Written English," address given at National Council of Teachers of English conference, Seattle (November 1976). Text transcribed and selected from the talk as delivered.

From a Class on Poetry

Every person in class is asked to keep track of experiences which relate in any way to poetry—sounds, images, overheard remarks—whatever.

Look for words which have *resonance* (in meaning) in Emily Dickinson.

The adjective is today our enemy. Salesmen, politicians, *soliciting* phonies over-use them: today's writers preserve austerity about them; e.g., Dickinson's "I heard a fly buzz"—how far do you read into the poem before you reach an adjective?

There is a pernicious idea that rhythm in poetry is scannable only: example—mechanical creations that fail; use mood-creating poems like Dickinson's "Hope is the thing with feathers"—something about the pace of this poem enforces a feeling. Look for later examples in the book of this ghostly effectiveness of rhythm more subtle than the scansion kind of pattern.

Robert Frost. In our day we do not people the landscape with spirits, but the kinds of places and the natural influences which at one time called forth or located spirits still exist: how do we react to the converging influences of our experiences—weather, seasons, gravity, day-night, etc.? An utterance which mentions these imagination-prodding things has power.

Wallace Stevens. There is a kind of guardedness in Stevens: he may be a New England American too sophisticated to like his mold but too inhibited to break out of it. His strategies may be ways of examining his plight, and may also be manifestations of it.

What if we could make a class—say, this one—be simply an extension of the lives we happen to be living: writings, experiences, discoveries—all brought to some order and vividness via a set, a sequence, of meetings? Really, that is what a class is, maybe; but we usually assume that the center of the endeavor is in the course material. It is in our lives.

William Carlos Williams is doing what the class was asked to do: find the poetry experience in the life we lead. By selection and sequence of the ordinary and universal to perceive the power of the common life around us.

Ezra Pound—how to save a culture by means of art. Pound is force rhetoric, abrupt: to convince, to persuade. Marianne Moore is evasion rhetoric: assumes sophisticated, friendly audience.

Recognizing Poetry in Everyday Experiences
Keeping a journal of everyday experiences which for any reason remind you of poetry—or art-experience in general—can serve several purposes. Any literature class deals quantitatively with these art-experiences: we survey some kind of spread of literary accomplishment, and unless we are realizing a certain quality of life in what we read we are not doing more than add aimlessly to our chance knowledge of heterogeneous materials. Twentieth-century literature invites close identification with the experiences of the writers, for they are like us, and we are able to approach very closely to their modes of operation. Further, to find out for oneself the ingredients of literature, via experiences that just *happen,* is to check and validate the concept of literature: it is to arrive empirically at the generalizations so convenient in considering and identifying literary effects.

Systems of *writing* the language are inadequate. Gerard Manley Hopkins tested the adequacy of writing and punctuation. Words and lines are not units in themselves—other larger complexes are units of utterance. He added notes on how to read his work, and used extra marks, for emphasis and so on.

To be with Yeats you often need commitment to one little simple idea: contemplating things of this world will bring a state of reverie which will indicate something *real*—a meaning, a truth, a vision. Where do you place—in your scheme of reality—those ideas, dreams, visions, imaginings which are, after all, existent but not easily accounted for? They exist more than if no one had imagined them—yes; what difference do they make? They are realms—*spiritus, anima mundi.*

But maybe Yeats is too oratorical . . .

Edward Thomas: What do you do if the values once held are a long time gone? If the sharp reactions to loss are over? If the individual religions (like Yeats's and Jeffers's) are themselves *old hat?* If excited denial has suddenly come to seem too much like affirmation? If you are no longer exhilarated by rebellion? If the pastness of the past is so evident as now to be just irrelevant?

How do you find your way then? (1) By immediate, small commitments. (2) By balanced, non-oratorical writings—and by non-oratorical lives.

Edward Thomas, D. H. Lawrence, Sylvia Townsend Warner, Robert Graves. What qualities in this set of people? Individual response, return to orthodoxy? Non-rhetorical: reduction of language. Minimum claims on glory. Totemistic-animistic impulse to get back in touch with animals, nature, the values of immediate experience. Some allegiance to man-in-relation-to-big-pattern (our rituals *mean . . .?*).

Auden. The use of myth, psychological materials; the sharp observation and political-rebel stance.

From teaching notes, Lewis & Clark College, Portland, Ore. (January–March 1960).

Farewell after a "Craft Lecture"

Fair winds. Go forth. Save up little pieces that escape other people—your dreams, the side glances your irresponsible mind makes, snatches of talk, whiffs from encounters. Pick up the gleanings.

And remember to be on guard against the routines you think you know, the forced commitments that you shun questioning.

Be careful of "craft."

III

Daily Writing

Three Poems on Writing

Writer in Residence

At first when I wrote it was daylight
in a room with others, and I was being
"a writer." Later I moved into a room
alone and sat by a window to look out.
But many distractions came, and I began
to get up early, before anyone moved.
My pen, though, made a noise. I found
smooth paper, and a quiet pen. Writing on
a solid board, by candlelight, in a room
by myself, I went inward for that silence
found only by moving where your thoughts
meet you, with no difference between the moment
and your easing forward with it as a silent
witness, carried wherever the world has to move.

Keeping a Journal

At night it was easy for me with my little candle
to sit late recording what happened that day. Sometimes
rain breathing in from the dark would begin softly
across the roof and then drum wildly for attention.
The candle flame would hunger after each wafting
of air. My pen inscribed thin shadows that leaned
forward and hurried their lines along the wall.

More important than what was recorded, these evenings
deepened my life: they framed every event
or thought and placed it with care by the others.
As time went on, that scribbled wall—even if
it stayed blank—became where everything
recognized itself and passed into meaning.

Adrift

Let my dream while I'm wide-awake
loose. Let me be drowned, baptized,
in the light given me. Day comes around,
night, fall, winter, spring,
summer. Leaves overhead, underfoot.
Waves arrive, buffets from friends
offended, enemies. Let it all come:
this is my way, this is the canoe I'm in.

———————

"Writer in Residence" (1975), from *The Small Farm;* "Keeping a Jour-
nal" (1985), from *An Oregon Message* (New York: Harper and Row,
1987) and *The Way It Is* (St. Paul: Graywolf Press, 1998); "Adrift" (1988),
unpublished.

Three Days, Four Poems

*An Interview with Vincent Wixon and
Michael Markee*

1: Journal Writing

Sometimes I think nothing is going to come out of a daily writing that I'm going to use directly at all. Though I must confess that what I feel the best about the writing is getting some resonance out of the language and also the incidents. There's a feeling that the language is enlarging or enhancing or somehow making more lively what I'm writing. I realize I have to confess that maybe more than what I'd like it to be, my journal writing is actually *writing,* actually creating something. But I like to feel relaxed about it, so I'm a little leery of being creative while I'm writing.

Do you think that your journal writing has changed over the years? If you look back at some of the early entries, did they turn more quickly into poems?

Well, recently I was feeling that not much was happening in my journal, whether I'm creating something or not creating something when I write, and I felt that the journal was pretty shallow, not very rich. So I went upstairs where I have stuff from years ago. I went back fifteen to twenty years or even farther and looked at my journals to see whether it seemed better to me then, which I assumed it would. I assumed there would be, more frequently, passes through areas of language that became poems or became something. What I found was, bad as my journal seems to me now, it seems even worse earlier. Which was sort of encouraging and I realized all over again that at least, according to my way of thinking, I shouldn't try to force these things, I shouldn't try to make my journal be good. I can't help making it good, I say, from years of practice, but I don't try to make it good.

So you don't think that you're, at least judging from your journal, more or less ambitious?

I was afraid that little lesson made me think I was becoming more ambitious, pressing. I don't know if this would seem significant to other people who write, but for me it's important to feel relaxed or ready to accept what comes. If I do that, then every now and then without trying, interesting things seem to come swimming along. That's the way it feels.

I was looking at an introduction to something recently where you said, "Each poem is a miracle that has been invited to happen." What kind of little prompts do you use to be receptive? I guess what I'm asking is what would be some typical things that would start you off in the morning writing?

I believe the little boosts that come, come from the writing itself and from the recollecting. I'm trying to back away from saying that there is any way to force this to happen. It's more as if something happens and I welcome its happening. So I begin to write it down. It isn't that I have a technique to make it interesting; it's that it's inherently interesting if I respond to the signals that the experience is giving me.

So when you start on a morning you don't say sometimes to yourself, "Well, what should I write about today? What's been interesting to me or what have I been thinking about?" You wait more for something to come to you?

It would seem like waiting, but you don't have to wait very long if your standards are low, you know. So you accept whatever comes along. Just yesterday I thought it might be fun to start with the last phrase I'd written the day before to see what more would come, and it did. It just sort of rolled over and the slant was a little different, but it started from the day before and I suddenly had this feeling, maybe I could write a whole series of things and the beginning of each would start from the end of the other. A new kind of chain. This may not seem like much but it was plenty to get me started writing.

You've talked about process a lot, but maybe you could say a little bit more about the importance of just writing rather than writing for an outcome.

Yes, I do hear quite a number of people saying the same thing. I can't tell whether I help induce it from others, but I can think of recent encounters with student groups in which we begin to talk about whether you're trying for excellence or you're determined to be a good writer or whether you're just accepting what comes, and they very often will begin to deny that they're trying to write good things, but I don't know whether I've induced that by the sort of atmosphere in the room or what. So I'm not sure that this is a lot different from what many people feel, but I can say categorically that for me it's significant. It's important to be accepting rather than to maintain some kind of standard when I'm writing. I don't know where the standard is as I'm writing, or maybe I'm just trying to go farther back in the process than most people go, because it is possible for me later to discard a lot of things I write. I certainly do that. I don't accept everything in the final product, but I think I accept everything in the initial product. I'll put it that way.

In my daily writing on November 22, 1989, a strange thing happens [*Reads from a sheaf of daily writings.*]

> In Argentina they have good faces.
> It's from living away off there toward
> the South Pole, and from having to
> learn Spanish. Besides, they have
> a lot to think about—their country
> tapering off that way, and winter coming,
> right when it's supposed to get warm.
>
> Some of them got mad at each other,
> like in other places we could name,
> and their heroes keep on being heroic
> and won't forget. Everyone tangos
> in the evening and talks about polo and that
> big bird—kind of a fake ostrich—
> running around over the estancia.
>
> Their national drink is a bitter tea
> mixed in a gourd, and they sip it
> all day, frowning their fine faces
> as they talk politics and gaze at the pampas.

Did you take that beyond the writing?

I don't think I did. I don't think I ever did anything with that.

It was too stereotypical a view of Argentina or . . .

I don't know. It seems sort of interesting to me now. I mean sort of a quaint . . . you think even the Argentines could forgive all that. Poor people, their country tapers off there on the map. Well, I might break my rule and go back to something. Maybe I can type it up and make it a poem.

Do you have a rule?

My rule is not to go back. It's more of a habit than a rule, because I don't feel any twinge about breaking it. It's just that I hardly ever go back. I just go on thinking something better, surely something better will come than this, surely.

Oh, there's more from the 22nd.

In a conversation you are flowing along, all OK. Then you say something, or act a certain way, or something else impinges on the flow, and suddenly the other person has changed, frozen somehow. What is it? You slow down; you modify what you just said; you switch to another topic. Nothing helps. There isn't any way to get back.

Later you may learn an offered explanation. But it may not really explain. Breakdowns are a condition of talk. Misunderstandings—or understandings?—will happen again, expected or unexpected. There is no way for a moving body, or mind, to avoid making mistakes. And staying still might be the worst mistake of all.

Well, I just abandoned that. Here's the 23rd of November. It has a title at the top that certainly came after it was all written down since Thanksgiving.

Thanksgiving

Apples are smooth as ever, and pears, hazel nuts.
Woodpeckers hard at work, rabbits meditating. Sunlight
slants through the woods; birdcalls bloom into sound
then fade. The forest stands, every leaf in place.

> At first in my life, the people around, were they
> real? At any minute the whole show might end,
> and that still might happen. But having the smooth
> birdcalls and the still leaves helps.

> Because the windows are double-glazed, candles make
> two reflections, and at breakfast our two candles make
>   four.

> They wait by the meadow, stiff gray
> junipers that crept out from the forest
> and stayed. Their future stares at them
> down from the mountains, winter, miles,
> and the whole cold, sliding, austere scene.

That's the end of the 23rd. Shall I read the 24th?

Did any of that become anything?

It didn't become anything. I'm getting a strange feeling about this, because what I said earlier about going back and looking to see if I was writing better in those days, a feeling it was terrible . . . I have a feeling this is pretty good, you know. I can make something out of any of these pages.

So what makes you decide not to take something farther and then not to go back and look at it?

I know this may seem incredible but I think it's just how headlong I get. If there's something else that comes along, I jump on it. Then I jump on the next. I just leave them. Maybe if I got more desperate I'd finish more poems, but I feel so good writing that I just go on writing instead of going back and doing something with them. Typing it up, making those final little adjustments; that's not so much fun to me. I guess I'm just getting so much in the habit of following where the rabbit's going that I'm better at catching rabbits than I used to be. Maybe, I don't know.

This is very strange, but the first line, at least on November 24th seems strange to me.

> In my dream I could see the back of my head.
> The hair was long, black, straggly, not covering a
> bald area carefully combed over.

Will they indulge us, allowing our spirits
to sing? In the theater of their lives
will they dance a few steps with us in the wings?
When the spotlight shines, will it rove their faces?

First on the left wing turn and survey
what we lost, the muddy streets and wooden
buildings here and there in the rain;
then on the right wing slant far over
hills and forest, rich and new,
a world that would last, ours forever.
Now look down: where we are,
solid, here for the time, warm.

I realize if I could only be exact or *just* in what I say, I think I
could make this little passage illustrate how easy it is to write if
your standards are low. It's just left, right, left, right, letting those
things surface that seem to want to surface as you go. It's almost
as if, to put it a way that wouldn't be very happy for me, it's as if
you have a formula. You pay more attention to the formula than
the content.

But the content varies so much, just in the ones you've read. Some-
thing prompted poems you're writing about Argentina and then some-
thing about communication, and apples and trees.

Well that is strange and it may be that, because on the 24th,
maybe I really started with the dream, "In my dream I could see
the back of my head." That might have been it. I can't remem-
ber now whether I did have that dream. But sometimes I do and
the dreams aren't coherent. One night you have a dream and
the next night you have a dream that doesn't seem connected.

You know Pascal said, "If our dreams were coherent we
wouldn't know which were our lives and which were our
dreams." It almost sounds as if I don't know which is my life be-
cause it isn't coherent either, at least the writing part.

2: Creating "Over the Mountains"

The 24th, that's the day that "Over the Mountains" came. In
fact, the 24th was a pretty exciting day. There's something else

here at the top of a page which wasn't the beginning of November 24th. Because I'm so cheap I use all the paper; when I ended on the 23rd I had a half a page left so I started the 24th. Then I have a whole page. Then another page.

Breath, incoherent life, here I go . . . In the margin, which means I wrote the title after I had written the poem, it says, "Over Near Chemult" [first thoughts bracketed].

Maybe someone stumbles across that [boy] child
lost [long] weeks ago, now chilled and unconscious, but
    breathing.
Maybe a friendly wanderer saved the [boy] child
for awhile, but had to go on, and this is the end.

(The world we all came from reaches out; its trees
embrace, its rocks come down ready to cover
us again. Moss clings to the feet and climbs
carefully, protecting its own. It wants us back.)

Now people carry the [boy,] child, warm him,
"save him," they say. Then he stirs and opens his eyes.
He doesn't want what he sees. He closes his eyes.
[That] The slow tide of the forest takes him away.

This doesn't happen just once; it happens always
to the lost, to [the searchers and parents,] parents and
    searchers, [to you, to me.] to me, to you.

That's pretty close to the way it got typed out then, maybe the day after. What this suggests, to me, is that these little bursts of activity in the journal get written out and every now and then one of them feels coercive enough to me that I type it out. But sometimes when I look back at the journal I can't see why this one coerced me any more than "Argentina" did, or whatever just preceded it. Maybe there isn't any reason, maybe it's just that I happened to be at my typewriter, and this is in front of me so I type it out. It doesn't sound orderly. A note in the margin here says, "I am trapped by my own text." I don't know why it says that. Here's more from November 24, after "Over the Mountains."

If I keep some promising piece of my journal around for delayed revision, even this "colder" piece of my own writing begins to feel something like a text for translating. For again I am confronted by a discourse that is already formed.

So I begin to think about translating.

Translation feels like solving a puzzle, to me. It takes patience, trying one move, then another, comparing, perceiving what the trend becomes when this move or that one stays. Every step forward modifies all the earlier steps and also helps determine what comes later.

This process is something like what happens when you are writing your own original. Then you can flourish forward and be the author, can exercise absolute power of decision. But if you are translating you feel strongly impelled to check yourself and return constantly to a text established in its main line of development and available for your "creating" only in its immediate, moving zone of attention as you progress.

The translation mode of writing leads me to feel like a detective. That trend as the immediate text unfolds is subject to constant adjustment—"So *that's* what is happening." And with developing confidence I adjust myself to the apparent aim of the trend before me.

I don't know how coherent this seems to you, but that's what I was thinking about when I was thinking about translating, sort of comparing it to how it is to launch forth on your own. You don't have to go back and check whether you're doing it right. You know you're doing it right.

You're not consciously taking out the best to shape and send out?

Apparently I'm not. Maybe I'm just taking out what's most convenient, which would be a reflection on my laziness. That would be part of it. Or maybe I'm taking out what seems to me—maybe this is sort of like convenience—what seems to me what's most easily adapted to my concept of what editors I'm currently dealing with would like to see. It's not the same as being most central to yourself or somehow cleaving to quality of what you're writing. I'm distracted by opportunities to publish, by other parts of my life which infringe on that area of attention where I might have used it to shape something that seems promising, but I'm distracted from because I have to work in the garden or whatever. Maybe for everyone it's like this even if they don't know it.

So there's a writing side to it and a marketing side or being aware of the market?

I'll try to see if I can phrase that other part. There's the writing part which is a strange mixed-up swirl of stuff that has a coherence perhaps, but you can't perceive it at the time. And then there's the part that has more coherence because it is shaped by your habitual tone of the stuff you type up. It's as if you artificially restrict the variety of your writing by the necessities of ironing out pieces to send out. Maybe I could be a more interesting published writer if I were less adept about choosing these convenient chunks to send away. Maybe.

So maybe the real you, the wilder stuff, is still in those stacks of daily writings you have in the study.

Yeah, and I think there's something else. It might be that even the stuff that you have stashed away isn't as wild as you really are because those are the things that you took the trouble to write down, and the things that skipped aside might be fascinating. So maybe the process of writing that I'd be interested in would be acquiring the knack of allowing the rejected cornerstones to become the cornerstones. I'm getting into Biblical language, but allowing those things that do not seem to have immediate negotiable relevance to have their right place in the real valid economy of your life. They're there waiting, but they don't have big voices, so you don't call on them.

I think what I'm doing here is trying to locate in myself some kind of principle of selectivity in writing that could be better or worse, I mean is probably relevant to everybody's writing, everybody's thinking, everybody's talking. You pay attention to, you round out, and you allow quality to certain parts of your life. In writing, part of the fun of it is that you at least fleetingly touch on those parts that are not conformed, are not conforming to the requirements of the life around you. They're more interesting, they're the undercurrents. And if we look through a journal that is written as mine is, sort of hit and skip and sink into the depths when you can get frivolous enough to do it, to put it in a paradoxical way, then those elements that you touch on seem incoherent. But you can look back over your life and you realize why they're there. I write about the person across the mountains because the little boy was lost across the mountains. It was in the news in Oregon. Or I write about what people in Argentina are like with all that whimsy about the shape of their country and so on, partly because I glimpsed a book that talks about the disappeared ones, which has pictures of their interesting faces. But even when I'm writing about something as serious as the disappeared ones in Argentina, there's a lot of whimsy in what I write. You know, they're drinking a bitter tea out of a gourd and so on. You can see where that comes from, too—general knowledge, meeting a missionary who talks about it, and so on. But why does it adhere to my attention? It's a long mystery.

In everyone's life there's all this torrent of things happening and a writer . . . maybe one way to say it would be someone who pays attention, and close attention at least at intervals, to that torrent. Or a writer is not someone who has to dream of things to write, but has to figure what to pick up out of the current as it goes by. "In my dream I can see the back of my head." People have dreams all the time, so I write it down. Then after that I say something about how the hair is. You can see how this would just spin out from a dream.

So there are events that prompt poems, like external events and newspaper headlines about the boy over the mountains. And that happens for everyone.

It can't help happening. There are other things I'd like to think about for a minute. One is if in your life you preserve intervals for paying attention to those things going by in the current, then you fetch them out and there'll be some coherence, whether you try to make it that way or not. It just will be. But then there's something more. To be a writer, to carry it beyond the current, and beyond selection from the current to the forming of something that you send out as a piece of writing, there's that extra stage besides sifting it out. There is some kind of dawning realization that these pieces could go together this way or this way or this way. [*Stafford forming his hands into different shapes.*]

The current happens to everybody. The selection happens to some. And the crystallizing of the selection happens to a writer.

How come you're a writer?

I think you get excited about seeing that these things can happen and the fuzzy, partially realized things in your life can come into focus or crystallize. You'll have pieces of experience that are mutually interiorly reinforced. You can pick up a fluff of snow. Or you can make a snowball. Or a snowman. Or you can make an ice sculpture. And the continuity of this process is a part of your experience and so you keep on doing it.

And the process for you involves words. It's not painting.

For me it involves words. We're all experts with the language and that's available to us. More available than snow. And those quirks in it come at you from other people's talk, from your own reading, from your own mutterings . . .

Would you please read "Over the Mountains" in its final form?

Yes, this is the way "Over the Mountains" turned out to be when I typed it out to send away for publication.

> Maybe someone stumbles across that child
> lost weeks ago, now chilled and unconscious but breathing.
> Maybe a friendly wanderer saved the child
> for awhile, but had to go on, and this is the end.
>
> (The world we all came from reaches out; its trees
> embrace; its rocks come down ready to cover
> us again. Moss clings to the feet and climbs
> carefully, protecting its own. It wants us back.)
>
> Now people carry the child, warm him;
> "Save him," they say. Then he stirs and opens his eyes.
> He doesn't want what he sees. He closes his eyes.
> The slow tide of the forest takes him away.
>
> (This doesn't happen just once; it happens again and again,
> to the lost, to searchers and parents, to you, to me.)

When I look at this I see how it alternates between a beginning quatrain that has particulars about that child, then has a quatrain, a kind of a generalization. "The world we all came from reaches out," how "its trees embrace" and so on. Then it has another particulars quatrain—"Now people carry the child, warm him," and so on. Then it has a final couplet that regeneralizes, saying this "doesn't happen just once; it happens again and again, to the lost, to searchers and parents, to you, to me." That seems the kind of standard pattern, maybe too standard. If I look at this I think OK, I had to do that last two lines as a kind of justification for my poem. Sort of drawing a lesson from it.

But I have a feeling of justification when I look at it again. I feel I've been bamboozled by current criticism into attacking my poem because that end, that last couplet is even more particular than the other parts of the poem. It takes this report and it hands it right to the reader. It's as if it's addressing the reader. This is not an event that's reported; it's an event that's happening to the reader. I'm just telling you, "This doesn't happen just once." It's as if I'm turning to the reader and saying, "Listen, you're not escaping this. You're in it."

I wanted to bring that event of that lost child people searched for for months, an event so dramatic for all of us in the Northwest, I wanted to make it be even more, to make the child not want to come back. Strange idea. "He doesn't want what he sees." There's another point of view. They say, "Save him." Actually the forest is saving him. Maybe this is a resurfacing of the old Greek saying of "What is best is not to have been born." One of those pessimistic old Greek dramatists. We don't think about that, but a writer thinks about what it's possible to think about. So I think of what, for me at least, surfaces in this poem is that those people are wrong. The forest, the forest has saved him. The forest takes him away. They're mistaken.

I don't know what kind of curl I have on the end where it says it happens to everyone. I guess it's sort of planked down at the end that this happens all the time. This was a tragic event. It's an inevitable event. It happened to this kid in this way. Somehow the nature of that event made me want to realize in writing, why did it grab us? It's just one thing that happened. All sorts of things happen, but somehow it gripped us. What is inside there? I think this poem teases some of it out.

And in stanza two, "The world we all came from reaches out; . . . It wants us back" is part of the heart of the thing. It's that the wilderness, which seems something we get lost in, is really a place where we belong. It's where we come from. "From the earth we came, to the earth we return." I guess that makes it not original by any means, but those things that are not original but haunt us through the centuries are lurking in incidents like this to be coercive of our feelings even when we don't know they're there.

There is some reason you focus on something. You don't have to know that reason, you don't have to mobilize it in words before you write, but it will show up in the course of the writing, and it will help confirm the value of human valence that an episode, incident, place, tone of voice or whatever had, that made it have coercion on you in the first place. That was waiting. For me that aspect of this experience was inherent in the experience. I didn't have to know it ahead of time. All I had to do was yield to my interest when I was writing.

Lostness is a function of your assumptions about where you belong. The ability to be lost is a precious thing for an artist. There's a knack for getting lost.

Can you talk a little about how you see the relationship of humans and other elements of nature? "The slow tide of the forest," the moss . . . Is there a way of talking about that in connection with this poem or other poems?

I'm afraid it's characteristic of me to be reaching out for those elements around us ordinarily subordinated to human life. I mean I even have a whole book called *Things That Happen Where There Aren't Any People*. I remember my impulse was to avoid the kind of writing that's human-centered all the time. I have this continual impulse to embrace with my thought and with my feelings more than human; to pay attention to dogs, to trees, to the wind, to shadows, to whatever, so I'm not surprised that I wander, I stumble, again and again into poems that have the forest doing something, the moss doing something, the rocks in this poem. It's all alive is my feeling and it's a mistake to stay just within human society with your attention.

Well, what is "over the mountains" then? What's over there?

Mysterious things, things we haven't control of, the cosmos. Not what we're able to manipulate, but what we are confronted with in our lives. There are things undreamt of. We are continually testing what's out there. Scientists do, religious people do. All of us do, I guess. I feel a very strong impulse in my own self to listen better, see better, read more, understand, "grok" what's going on.

This relationship with other things of nature besides people. In this poem it seems to be not menacing, it's claiming its own . . . "wants us back."

"It wants us back."

But you don't see nature as always like this, do you? Sometimes it's "The Animal That Drank Up Sound."

Yes it's true, at least in that poem, I have some life, taking it back, bringing back more life, more sound. I realize we've strayed into a kind of attempt to classify one specimen—me—as having a certain interest, but I think a writer is a person who is ready for any kind of interest. I'd like to be so available to points of view that I wouldn't be true to one view of nature. This is one poem; that's another poem. Nature goes silent and empty and is brought back by a little cricket. I like that idea too. I think a writer is a person who is ready for the adventure that what unfolds during the writing offers.

So we're back to going where the poem leads you.

Yes, it's much more various than having a philosophy or having a belief. You are ready to jettison any philosophy or any belief or even preference in the interests of some opening that you perceive while you're creating something. I think the fun of creating things is not that you're able to bolster what you already have, but you're ready to find things that you don't already have. When we analyze somebody's work, we keep trying to corner them—and that's all right, you can identify that. Maybe even somebody could identify it in me or any other writer. But the life of the writing is in the vulnerability of that impulse while you're creating something.

Ideally I would start all over again every morning to be back to neutral again as I start to write the next thing. I want to see where it's going to go. I realize that characteristically I drift in certain directions, I'm sure of that. But the positive part of creating is the nonorthodoxy, the unpredictability, the readiness to be different, even if difference means lack of quality. Because if you feel it has to be quality all the time, then you have to identify some kind of direction as quality.

How important is anonymity?

I have a strong impulse for anonymity. It may not seem like it when we're here talking, to record some talk, but if I had my druthers I'd disappear. I had this phrase before Bush did, "Read my lips, forget my name." I wanted to present things, but I didn't want to be the presenter. I mean I wanted to disappear. I think Joyce had this idea too. The whole idea of the disappearing author. Let the work do it. Come to think of it, Kierkegaard, who I've been reading, half the things he published were under other names.

Related to "Over the Mountains," is that part of the impulse?

Come to think of it, there's quite a bit of disappearing in this poem. A wanderer is gone, then the child is gone, taken away, and at the last, even ridding oneself of any distinction, saying this doesn't happen just once; it happens to the lost, the searchers, the parents, to you, to me. Not a distinction, but a blending is in this poem, I think.

You know, there's another thing about this poem. There are long and short sentences. I just thought of this as a general thing. Part of the fun of discourse, not just writing, but also talking, is that playing of elements, the variety. I was conscious of things like "It wants us back" at the end of the second stanza and "He closes his eyes" near the end of the third stanza as contrasts to longer things, such as "This doesn't happen just once; it happens again and again, to the lost, to searchers and parents, to you, to me." I mean those differences are part of the experience, the language experience of the poem.

And I was thinking that another kind of limber consideration in writing is connected to this poem. A critic might take a certain part of a poem and say this rhythm is not worthy. When you're a writer I think you fall into certain rhythms not on the basis of any abstract idea of what's a good rhythm or a bad rhythm, but how they go together, what context makes this OK. I think, for instance, having "It wants us back" and "He closes his eyes" in the same poem is a part of what establishes the basis of what this poem is. Is this staccato?—(I'm just trying for extreme statements)—or is it mellifluous, and so on. The feel of the whole poem justifies itself from the parts of the poem. You can't take a part out without changing the other parts.

It just occurred to me that there are things that you leave out of the poem—I mean things from the real event. The pony for example. In the news there was a lot about the pony that came back to camp.

I sacrificed breadth for penetration, I think by instinct. Last summer in a workshop someone said about a work by someone, "This could be tightened up." I'd heard this often. But this time I thought to stop everyone and say, "What does this mean to say it could be tightened up?" And this person said—it wasn't a challenge to enlighten me—"What I mean is there's a part of this poem that makes an excursion about something it doesn't need to do. The writer could leave this part out and still get where she's going." So we talked about that for awhile. I did understand "tighten it up." But I said, "But what if what you've taken out isn't really peripheral. It's crucial, or it's as significant as anything else." Then we saw that tightening up isn't always good. Sometimes you want to loosen up. I winced a little bit when you said the pony could be in there. I thought, yeah, I could loosen it up and maybe I'd enrich my poem. It would be a different kind of poem. This one just zeroes in on the boy doesn't want to be saved. I didn't even think about loosening it up and having the pony, and I want to be able to do everything. [*Laughs.*]

Back to structure, I think of a famous poem like "Traveling through the Dark" which is also in quatrains. So there are real formal elements to "Over the Mountains."

Yes there are, that's true. I think that such formal elements are reassuring to a writer. I like the opening and closing of parts of a complete thing, the whole. There's a whole. There are parts; they are whole. And there's a kind of reassurance for me in closing it up, opening it up, closing it, opening it, closing it, opening it. That just happens to be the attention span of a reader or something like that.

Also, there's that "friendly wanderer" in the first part of the poem. I have a feeling that the friendly wanderer is needed as a possible way for this child to have survived longer than the searchers could believe. This is how it got into the poem. After a week or so the searchers were not really confident that the child was alive, but if there had been a wanderer, say someone camping, the child would have stayed with them, he could easily be alive. But then that wanderer saved the child and had to go on, so the child could have been in the wilderness for a lot longer time.

So the wanderer's friendly, but has its own demands?

Other things to do. Now I begin to like the title "Over the Mountains." It's a kind of phrasing that without calling attention to itself, epitomizes the poem. You go over. This is like "going West." It's like disappearing. It's like something that happens in another place. There is another place in this poem, and that's where the child goes. Even that line that says, "The slow tide of the forest takes him away"—that's what happens to the child. The first title "Over Near Chemult" implies the poem's going to be somehow related to that town near where it really happened, but that's too specific. Actually it's about what happens in the wilderness to a lost child, and then maybe it's also about what happens to all of us.

The end of the first stanza, "and this is the end."

That sort of anticipates, doesn't it. Because it declares that this is the end while the child is still sort of alive. Do the people warm the child later? "'Save him,' they say." It turns out not to be true. I guess I mean when I say "and this is the end," this is the result. Here's the child unconscious, chilled, but breathing. One of the things I like to do in this poem is to start out with speculation, *maybe*, "*Maybe* someone," "*Maybe* a friendly wanderer." Then after that it's just the way it is: "Now people carry the child, warm him; 'Save him'. . . . he stirs." No more maybe about it. I'm in the realm of the poem so I just stay there.

Well that way of beginning is pretty "Staffordian." Don't you think that "maybe this happened" is a kind of stance you often take?

My world has a lot of maybe in it. I don't know if I've said this to you before, but when I was up in Alaska some linguistics person up there said, "Your language is like the Eskimo language. The way you talk is like Eskimos." I said, "What do you mean?" This person said that when the Eskimos talk they have a lot of maybe. They live in that kind of environment where maybe something, maybe not. So if you say to someone, "Shall we go hunting tomorrow?" their response in their language has this kind of element in it: "We might go hunting tomorrow, maybe, if the weather is right." There are a number of exits because you're not sure if you can go hunting tomorrow or if there is a tomorrow, or if we'll still want to go hunting. So your response is

116

congenial, but indefinite. And I think I have a lot of that—a lot of the feeling of the indefiniteness of most people's certainties.

Even in a recent poem, "What's in My Journal," you write, "Somebody's terribly inevitable life story, maybe mine."

"Maybe mine." That's right. I don't know if this is a distinction or not, certainly not an honorific distinction, but I believe that my characteristic stance toward experience is that it's much more unpredictable than most people say.

When you were reading the draft of "Over the Mountains," you were also reading changes that you made. Did you make those changes while you were writing that same morning?

"Maybe someone stumbles across that boy." "That boy"—that's the way I had it. When I changed it to "child," it was probably after I'd written through it, but it's on the same text because I just go back and begin to have a kind of a feeling. I guess I changed it from "boy" to "child" for a number of reasons. I wanted it to be young, helpless, and inclusive. But I would give that up, the desire for inclusiveness or youngness, for other considerations if there were some. And when it says in the second line, "lost long ago," I wanted to give some sense of the duration. It was a long time ago, weeks ago. The strange thing to me is that so little got changed.

That's not typical?

When I look at something like "Argentina," I probably wouldn't change that a lot. There'd be little changes, but not a lot of changes. Here's one way to put it. Maybe if I think of making a poem it'd be like knapping a flint arrowhead. You'd have a lot of pieces, and you'd start on one, and you'd have a pretty good run going, and you're going to finish an arrowhead, but if it's the wrong thickness or an odd kind of piece or has a hidden flaw in it or something, then you give up. So maybe the ones I send out—I'm sort of back to what I've said before—it seems like convenience, but it may be necessity. For me at least, for my way of writing, that if it's coming out right while I'm writing it, that helps me write it right the rest of the way. It's like making an arrowhead, and it's going to be finished. Some of the others might be wonderfully promising pieces, but something may begin to go wrong and I skip that part. I mean I don't go back and make a knife out of it instead of an arrowhead. I just cast it. I'm making arrowheads. Arrowheads is what the editors buy, but God might like these other things better.

So in a sense you're not as interested in revising as in creating.

It may be what other people call revising I accomplish by just starting farther back and running through it again. Some may feel what they write down they need to stay with and finish. I have more of a feeling that what I write down there's going to be a lot more in my life, and if it doesn't feel happy today to finish this, I'll take another run. And so it's not the deliberate decision not to do the work on something you've done; it's more like being enticed by the next thing than being abidingly locked into the last thing.

It does feel like a kind of recklessness, like a profligacy. There's all these things, all these pieces of flint I can make arrowheads out of and I'm willing to have them be different shapes or something like that. It's strange, and there's another level in that, I think. Whatever you write down is a part of your life, is a part of the experience of your life that may be better realized by another thing that you write down. So the important thing is not to make something of everything you write, or not to always have something that other people will like, including editors, but somehow in your writing to have an experience that is concurrent with other needs in your life so that your writing is not the making of negotiable poems. It is staying in the current of your life. If that current takes me somewhere else, that's where I'm going to go. I'm not going to come back here and eddy around in order to have a picture of this part of the journey. I'm going to make the journey.

It might seem that "Over the Mountains" didn't change much from how it came out on the page, so one might say this poem wasn't revised much, but there's another aspect of this, and that is how much it's revised before it gets on the page. How about those instantaneous million revisions while you're writing? What enables a writer to have lines that break helpfully at places that are approximately equal down the page? Why aren't some lines one word long, others clear over to the other side? How does it happen, that alternation that's in this—and it was in the original draft—between a particular and a general thing?

How does that happen that those blocks are self-consistent? There must have been internal revisionings during the writing. So to ask someone if they've revised and to judge if they're telling the truth or not by how many marks they make on their page after they write it down may be to enter the process too late to catch the most crucial revisions. What if someone could be so used to writing or talking, and we all are used to that at least, that they would talk formed units? And in a way we do when we talk sentences. So that idea of revision is internalized, instantaneous, and maybe crucially accomplished during the first writing down for some people.

I've been writing more than fifty years, I suppose. It wouldn't be surprising, would it, that a lot of that revisioning is internalized as it goes down on the page. Perhaps from our reading, from some of these journal entries earlier it might be even discouragingly assumed that I just write down poems. I had that feeling when I was reading that thing about Argentina. What's the use of revising if they're already perfect? That would be one way of looking at it. Well, of course, they're not already perfect, but they may be very close to what my best utterance would be on second thought.

Maybe a lot of this is internalized, and if I go back and look at those things that I wrote when I was beginning to write, I would see more of what would appear to be blundering and less of the writing of it in a way where it doesn't have to be drastically revised after the first version. I'm not sure this is true; I don't have any feeling of change and even if I had changed, I wouldn't be sure that was good. I like the idea of awkwarding into the poem, rather than being so inhibited or so trained that I can't do those helpful blunders that bring about unexpected things. I shy away from learning how, but maybe I have learned how. I'm afraid if you learn how too well you won't do those surprising things that are the most fun in writing.

I've had that feeling I could take anything I've written and just turn it into a diamond by revision. You know, put enough pressure on it that it would crystallize. I haven't searched around to find some hopeless thing and then actually turned it into a diamond because I've been distracted by things that are already partly diamonds. That's the feeling I have, that it doesn't make any difference what you start out with; it's what you end with that counts.

To end with "Over the Mountains," the poem isn't just about the event.

No, the ostensible topic is this. The grip-on-the-people topic is why this means something to them. My poem must—I'm trying to extrapolate from this about writing in general—my poem must use local materials in such a way as to make them resonate with whatever it is that makes people focus on those local materials in this way. I didn't think about that when I wrote it. But maybe, it suddenly occurs to me, maybe part of the knack of writing is to present local materials in such a way as to have them get that hook on prevalent human concerns. It might be that I might be groping toward something like archetypes, something like that.

Are you getting at what you want in the poem?

When we verbalize about the writing process we make it sound as if the writer gropes around to find what these relevances are. But as a writer I feel all I do is lend myself to the feelings in this local event and the nature of my life will force those relevances on me. I don't have to search for them. All I have to do is give myself to the feelings of the local event and the archetypal resonance will appear. I was not deliberately yoking this lost child to a perception of what it is to be lost or to be saved, but our interest in that lost child comes about through the lurking presence of that abiding concern we all have about what it means to be lost or saved.

I don't have to be smart. I don't have to be alert. I just have to be victimized by the event. Or maybe victimized isn't the word, but I have to lend myself fully to significances that emerge. Not through my management, but through my susceptibilities.

Portions of this interview were used in *William Stafford: The Life of the Poem* (TTTD Productions, 1992), videocassette. Part 1: "Argentina" (November 22, 1989), "Thanksgiving" (November 23, 1989), and "In my dream I could see the back of my head" (November, 24, 1989) are all unpublished. Part 2: "Over the Mountains" (November 24, 1989) is from *The Long Sigh the Wind Makes* (Monmouth, Ore.: Adrienne Lee Press, 1991) and *The Way It Is* (St. Paul: Graywolf Press, 1998).

Four Early Poems

"Vacation," "Fall Journey," "Traveling through the Dark," "Back Home"

A Crash of Dissonant Life

Vacation

One scene as I bow to pour her coffee:—

> Three Indians in the scouring drouth
> huddle at a grave scooped in the gravel,
> lean to the wind as our train goes by.
> Someone is gone.
> There is dust on everything in Nevada.

I pour the cream.

"Vacation" is short, but it could unfold forever.

You know how it is when you are doing something, and a little incident comes along, and you can't stop what you are doing, but that incident balloons out and stays with you? The thing you are doing at the time requires your attention, and no one else can realize that the main current of your life has slipped aside and found something suddenly important. But you have to disguise that discovery.

When our train went by a windy, dry place, I saw some people standing by a grave. Just a glimpse I had—a piece of life given me and then snatched away. They were so still, and the wind buffeted them so, and the world stretched out around them, so lonely—and gone . . .

We on the train were elegant—warm, easy, ready to dine. The

form it all took was just as it came to be in my poem: a glance out, a crash of dissonant life, and a calm (an apparently calm) return to our elegance.

Everyone else on our side of the train glimpsed the scene, too. It was only a graveyard, one of those blank enclosures in the desert with a few stones propped. And the hot wind was blowing, and our train itself made a wind and a clatter and a distraction to the unfortunate people out there trying to hold themselves secure and upright and significant. Enjoying our vacation, we blinked aside and then erased and forgot—almost—the stab of reality.

In the kind of art I do, my job at this point is easy to summarize, but endlessly difficult to perform right. I must accept the given elements in my experience and then allow them to interact. I also have available certain tricks or powers; for instance, I can appear to be artless. I can scatter my little poem abruptly before the reader, with very little elaboration. The poem itself can be a glimpse "out the window."

And, oh, it is lucky for me that at the end I can "pour the cream," so rich, so soothing. Or is it soothing?

My mood endures long after the poem is over, and is renewed even to now. And I don't even have to tell you any more about it.

It is part of myself that I am keeping.

Converging of Evidences

Fall Journey

Evening came, a paw, to the gray hut by the river.
Pushing the door with a stick, I opened it.
Only a long walk had brought me there,
steps into the continent they had placed before me.

I read weathered log, stone fireplace, broken chair,
the dead grass outside under the cottonwood tree—
and it all stared back. We've met before, my memory
started to say, somewhere. . . .

And then I stopped: my father's eyes were gray.

In this poem the ingredients begin to shift toward some kind of meaning. Evening is "a paw." (I want that paw to appear gray, but cannot say so at first.) The person in the poem is cautious. He is walking into a continent placed before him. All things begin to try to say something, and the sights are gray—weathered log, stone, old furniture, dead grass, and a cottonwood tree, which has silvery gray bark and steadfastly populates even the dry country in western parts of the United States. This poem is one of the odder ones which has occurred to me; it becomes a converging of evidences up to a point and then just a break, a break, because the evidences have clicked into the message. In a rush, the cautious experiencer in the poem reads the world placed before him, and what he sees is what he has carried to this point in his journey, a memory of his father's eyes.

Actually, I was thinking of a place on the Arkansas River, and the grass, and the sky . . . so, I walked into that poem, gray, gray, gray, and then the end came to me, as a result of it. I said, "Oh, it all comes back. My *father's eyes* were gray." And someone gave me a word for it once. At a poetry gathering, a woman came up and said, "You know that poem of yours, 'Fall Journey'? That is called—" And then she had a psychological term for that, sort of like, you know, it all comes together, like some kind of Rorschach. You know, God's Rorschach test. And He says, "Gray." Oh, yeah. Yeah, *that's* the key. . . . Yes, and you make me see something about this that I hadn't noticed, and that is that in a way, where we say something doesn't follow, and so the end of the poem seems like a leap; it's just because—one way to put it would be, just to try to establish a point, we have been paying attention to the wrong sequence. The poem is in the right sequence, all right, but it's a surprising sequence that you don't realize until you get there. You don't realize what the principle has been. It's almost like math, or music, and so what comes at the end is inevitable, if you put the right overlay on the poem. But you've been reading it with a different overlay in mind. I'm just dreaming this up as I go, but, yes, it follows.

Five Footnotes to "Traveling through the Dark"

Traveling through the Dark

Traveling through the dark I found a deer
dead on the edge of the Wilson River road.
It is usually best to roll them into the canyon:
that road is narrow; to swerve might make more dead.

By glow of the tail-light I stumbled back of the car
and stood by the heap, a doe, a recent killing;
she had stiffened already, almost cold.
I dragged her off; she was large in the belly.

My fingers touching her side brought me the reason—
her side was warm; her fawn lay there waiting,
alive, still, never to be born.
Beside that mountain road I hesitated.

The car aimed ahead its lowered parking lights;
under the hood purred the steady engine.
I stood in the glare of the warm exhaust turning red;
around our group I could hear the wilderness listen.

I thought hard for us all—my only swerving—,
then pushed her over the edge into the river.

1

I don't believe that the most profitable way to become a writer is to seek intense experiences. If you write, things will occur to you. The activity of writing will make things occur to you in your mind. You write the documentary that you think, rather than the documentary that you live. When you write, it doesn't make so very much difference what you have done, or intend to do, but it makes quite a bit of difference what occurs to you at the moment you're writing. It's an inventive kind of thing. The feeling in writing is not relying on experience before, but relying on a kind of sense of immediacy now while you're writing. It's not so much that it's built up inside of you, it's just as if you have a readiness to respond to what occurs to you at the moment. I can't really tell how much that reservoir has to do with the writing. I think it's that willingness to go along with what occurs to you at the moment that's more important than any buildup of previous experiences.

The experience of writing "Traveling through the Dark" was not that of deciding to communicate to the world about a condition it was in. For me, it was encountering in myself some kind of developing feeling as I went along writing the poem. It wasn't programmed to an external situation, but it was meeting a developing possibility in my own mind when I wrote it. After it's done I like the idea that it might appeal to others, that it might connect with ideas they have, but the process of writing it, for me, is not anticipating what they want, but following out how I feel.

2

I do think it's an easy kind of poem. You can learn how to do a poem like that. In fact, I think there are a lot of poems like that. And so it's more like the sort of writing you can do, and you can do a job, and you can be clear, and you can go straight toward the ending, and it does have a sense of direction throughout the poem in a kind of trajectory. Still, there are other poems I've written that retain my interest much more than that one does simply because it is so neat. And I can imagine a critic saying it's one of those obvious . . . you know, I was there, I saw it, I'm telling you kind of poems. . . . I remember taking it to a writers' group we had in town. We met down in the Portland Library, as I remember. We sat around a table, and it came my turn to read what I'd done this week. I read "Traveling through the Dark." And there was a catch of breath and they all said, "No, no, Bill, you can't end it that way!" That's when I thought, that's exactly what I'm going to do, end it right there. And so I just gave up revising it anymore and sent it out.

3

The things that occur to you. You know, you start to tell someone something. There are some things you think are more worth telling than others. You get home and someone says, "What happened?" You start to tell them. Sometimes you don't know why it is that this seems important to you, but if you start to tell it, and then you tell the things that make you feel a certain way about it, it begins to be more. That's what writing is. You say something, and then something else adds to it.

4

Let me confess—I didn't really push the deer into the river. I guess that was poetic license, and I hope I didn't induce anyone else to do so reckless an act!

Over the years I have suffered a number of criticisms for my poem—some of them from people who thought I was too sentimental and shouldn't have even thought about *doing something* for the deer or the fawn.

Let's be good citizens. I'll try to do my part.

5

One thing I would say is that the assumption that something can be done in extreme circumstances like that is the assumption that neglects the difference between real time and effective time. That is . . . well, you know the idea of the "specious present"? This is the idea that something is going on to the point at which nothing is going to change it, and you feel, it hasn't happened yet, therefore, there's something that can be done, but in effect it's already happened. And the example I heard someone say is, you're standing on board the Queen Mary. It's going full speed. About fifty yards from the dock the captain turns to you and says, "You take over." According to some people's way of thinking, OK, there's still time to do something. But the captain knows and you know and God knows there's no time. It's all over. So it was all over for the deer.

So, if I were talking to students and we had a lot of time, we could talk about the specious present. And there are people who kid themselves all their lives about this, and there are some others who know that there are openings and closures of opportunity that are like a steel trap. You can kid yourself if you want to, but if you don't want to, how about doing something else? . . .

I've had trouble with people in political discussions about pacifism, and so on. I remember once taking a stand: well, I can't stop war. Jesus couldn't stop war. Eisenhower couldn't stop war. Why should I blame myself for not stopping war? What I can do is, to do the things that are within my power. I can decide there's one person who won't be in it. That's a possibility. But I can't stop it, and someone who was there kept saying, "Well that answer's not good enough for me." You know, he had this John Wayne reaction: "I'm going to stop it." That leads you to terrorist acts that don't really do any good, but they relieve your conscience. I don't want to relieve my conscience; I want to do good.

Drastic Final Image: "Back Home"

Back Home

The girl who used to sing in the choir
would have a slow shadow on dependable walls,
I saw. We walked summer nights.
Persons came near in those days,
both afraid but not able to know
anything but a kind of Now.

In the maples an insect sang
insane for hours about how deep the dark was.
Over the river, past the light on the bridge,
and then where the light quelled at limits
in the park, we left the town,
the church lagging pretty far behind.

When I went back I saw many sharp things:
the wild hills coming to drink at the river,
the church pondering its old meanings.
I believe the hills won; I am afraid
the girl who used to sing in the choir
broke into jagged purple glass.

A person who has moved away from a little town where he lived as a young man has gone back for a visit, and while there he has remembered a girl he used to know. This girl was a certain kind, good, young, steady, and subjected along with the young man to the trance-like summer influences which the poem tries to evoke: it was a wonderful time and a terrible time, and the recollection of it is almost unbearably intense. It is that combination of goodness, and danger, and beauty—and absolute loss—which I want to conjure with my admittedly drastic final image: jagged purple glass. I hope the image is justified by many things in the poem—the church windows implied, the lights and shadows, the sharp things, the fear. As a construction, I hope that the poem carries itself off by means of the deliberately narrative movement and by its three-part development. The stanzas will serve my purposes if they impose any general sense of recurrence, even just because they are about the same length—no rigorous pattern is wanted: I would prefer that the reader be enticed along by gentle displacements and sufficiently frequent verbal events, even such slight ones as having to rove from line two to line three to pick up the ending of the first sentence: "I saw." I want that reader to stroll with increasing vividness through the summer nights of a small town, and then into the intensity of the final realization. No? It doesn't work? I suppose not—but oh how I'd like to make it do so!

When I hear this hanging in the air, after saying it, "broke into jagged purple glass," I have several feelings, and one of them of guilt occurs to me. Just the idea that it might seem that writing is done by figuring out something striking, and I wouldn't like to think of it that way. It happens, but it's not so satisfying as other things. What I'm afraid of is it will seem as if we're trying for certain local, granulated effects.

This is from back a little way in my writing. I remember I felt pretty good about the ending—"broke into jagged purple glass." That's the way to do it, I thought. But afterward, other things began to come to me and because I know how to do that I began not to believe in it. Once you've got the formula, that's not it anymore. It's something else.

"Vacation" (1950), from *The Hudson Review, West of Your City* (Los Gatos, Calif.: The Talisman Press, 1960), and *The Way It Is* (St Paul: Graywolf Press, 1998). The commentary appeared in *Literary Cavalcade* (March 1986).

"Fall Journey" (1954), from *Prairie Schooner, Traveling through the Dark* (New York: Harper and Row, 1962), and *The Way It Is* (St. Paul: Graywolf Press, 1998). Commentaries: "In this poem . . . ," response to *Critical Quarterly* questionnaire (August 1964); "Actually, I was thinking . . . ," from *Roving Across Fields,* ed. Thom Tammaro (Daleville, Ind.: The Barnwood Press Cooperative, 1983).

"Traveling through the Dark" (1956), from *The Hudson Review, Traveling through the Dark* (New York: Harper and Row, 1962), and *The Way It Is* (St. Paul: Graywolf Press, 1998). Commentaries: "I don't believe . . . ," from an interview on WBOE radio, Cleveland, Ohio (March 14, 1969); "I do think . . . ," from "'Traveling through the Dark': An Interview with William Stafford," by Vincent Wixon and Michael Markee, *Oregon English* (autumn 1989); "The things that occur . . . ," from a reading to schoolchildren in San Rafael, California (May 10, 1967); "Let me confess . . . ," from a letter to Tom Dalgliesh (November 6, 1989); "One thing I would say . . . ," from Steven Hind, "An Interview with William Stafford" [typescript], conducted February 6, 1984, published in *Cottonwood* (fall 1984).

"Back Home" (1957), from *Northwest Review, The Rescued Year* (New York: Harper and Row, 1966), and *The Way It Is* (St. Paul: Graywolf Press, 1998). Commentaries: "A person who has moved away . . . ," response to *Critical Quarterly* questionnaire (August 1964); "When I hear this . . . ," from a reading at Ruth Steven Poetry Center, Tucson, Ariz. (February 21, 1968); "This is from back a little way . . . ," from a reading at Butler County Community College, El Dorado, Kans. (November 5, 1986).

On Revision

An Interview with Vincent Wixon and Michael Markee

Revision is something that comes up often in discussions wherever I go, writers' workshops and so on. It often comes up in my own brooding about what I'm about when I'm writing. And often I've found myself at odds with others in discussing it because I sound so welcoming to whatever occurs to me when I'm writing. I am, and I want to be. But also that welcome could extend to things that occur to me after I've written. Or later in the same phase of writing something may occur to me in the same session, and I go back, because something suddenly occurs to me that I could do, or some turn I could take. Or I could have started in a different place, or given it a different emphasis. So I like to feel available for any kind of hunch that comes when I start to write, but also available for any further hunches and changed hunches that occur. So being open to revision is to me like being open to the availability of being creative when you first start.

Every time around I think of something else. What I think of this time, though, is that there is a difference between that first plunge through material when you're writing and those alternative thoughts that occur to you after you've gone through it once. Somehow they are more regular, more reliable; you feel that they are more connected with people who are likely to be venturing into what you've written. You are able to go back and do a kind of double thinking through it—that is, your own impulses plus the anticipated impulses of others. So it's possible that you can curry your own thoughts in a different way the second time through.

The first time, you know you're blundering along. I mean you want to recognize anything that shows up. But the second time there are some things you've learned you shouldn't recognize because they're going to intrude on whatever the main drift of your discourse this time is going to be. So there's an ordering part to revision.

The first time through your audience is yourself, and the second time through you're thinking of another audience, or extending your audience?

Well, I think what has always made me wary of agreeing with people who want to be firm revisioners is that I don't want to change my perceptions in order to accommodate other people. Somehow it would seem demeaning of the other people. After all they can have thoughts like mine and maybe a lot better. So why should I try to curry this out? But what I suddenly glimpse this time is that in a way you yourself have changed as an audience the second time through. You are a more informed audience. You anticipate getting to someplace that you have glimpsed the first time through. So when you go through the next time there may be adjuncts to thoughts; there might be a lot to be added. You see further opportunities the next time through, and the first time through is a deliberately wandery kind of search out and explore. The second time through you are bolstered by your recollection of what were the dead ends the first time through, and so you can just do it better. It'd be like going through a thicket the second time. There were some misturnings that you wouldn't do the second time, and you could take advantage of certain parts of the trail that you'd established.

So revision keeps on being creative. But it's creative in a little bit different way. You yourself are a more sophisticated audience the second time through. That would help me keep from trying to distort what I had to give in favor of my idea of either how bright or how stupid the audience is. So I'm the audience, but I'm a different audience. And I'm a more sophisticated audience the second time through. Does this seem to make any difference?

It does. You talk often about opportunities. Can you think of particular examples in revision, or opportunities that come along that could illustrate?

Yes. For one thing, even when I was talking then . . . I can't remember exactly how I said it, but I said that the first time through you're wandering around, a kind of discovery. Even that second thing I said was a sudden realization that I got a multisyllable word I could use here that embodies everything—you're kind of wandering along, you're discovering. In other words, the language itself yields to you a more efficient way to say something that you've started to say with a kind of a tentativeness. And you suddenly realize that there is available for you in language a more direct, a more evocative way to say it. Instead of "kind of wandering around," you say "discovery."

But in taking these opportunities and wandering around in language, what are you trying to discover?

What I'm trying to discover is what the world is presenting to me today in the conditions it has and conditions I have. It's a kind of mutuality between the outside and the inner world. I think that's what I'm trying to discover.

When you're writing or revising, do you think in terms of language or content?

I can't really tell. I think for someone who has learned to talk that connection is so immediate I can't catch it. I can't catch the difference. I just can't feel a lag between maybe something that's going on before language and language itself. Language is there. Maybe it is even the instigator of some of those things we think of. It's a mysterious thing, language.

It would seem then that in some ways you're a patient writer. I mean you're not in any hurry to send poems off or get them to a certain point. You can wait for other things to come.

At least I like to be in the situation where nothing outside of me hurries me. Sometimes I feel impetuous when I think I've got something. You know, I'm ready to do something with it. And sometimes I've been really fast in writing something and sending it out. I ought to feel guilty, from what people tell me about keeping it around and improving it. I'm far from saying it couldn't be improved, but sometimes I'm so delighted I send it away. But if there is somebody else rushing me, something happens in my process, and I do it a different way. Because of my eagerness to please, if someone gives me a deadline, I'm likely to do it at least by the deadline or earlier, since I think they're in a hurry. But that means closing it out on the basis of a process that's different from the slow mature-on-the-vine kind of writing. You know you can force the product and give it a closure and send it out. And I can do that on deadline, but the deadline that's in my head is not a deadline. It's more like a lifeline. It's more like a hope. So if you do something and then if you feel as I do, if you feel exhilarated by what you've already done, part of the exhilaration is there could be more, you know. And so all sorts of revisings outward occur to you.

Actually I have to begin to limit that. A fusion of possibility in the interest of doing other things, too. I mean your whole life could be taken up by this thing that gets exciting. Sometimes I've felt too glib. Many times I've felt too glib about ending something. So if I were counseling with someone else about it, say at a writers' conference or something like that, and they wanted to hold off, I would say, "Yeah, hold off as long as you can." But my life has been such that I've often brought things around and given a little neat fold and tied them with a bow and sent them out into the world without enough revision.

Has the way you revise changed drastically over the years?

It drags me a little bit to say this, but I think of late, in the last two or three years, something has happened in revision. Partly it is that I don't feel the impulse so much to send things out, and that means sometimes these things hang around. They're just lounging around home for a long time and not getting out and earning a living. I'll go on to something else, and I don't go back to them.

It used to be, it sort of went click, click, click. I couldn't rest once I had something I thought could be something; I had to make it be something. I can remember writing something one night and sending it out the next morning. Now I have something I think could be something, well, why do anymore about it for awhile? Something else may happen. So maybe, just through lack of momentum, I'm turning into one of those good people I was always told to be, to keep things around longer, maybe you'll improve them enough that they might be worthy of publication.

You talked once about looking at poetry you'd written years ago, and how this would be almost as if it were written by another person. Do you ever feel the impulse to go back to revise something you've written ten years ago?

I always feel that I could revise it just as I always feel I could translate, but it's not the same feeling. Something that's fairly recent I could revise without feeling I'm translating. The recent things are still trying to be something in my mind. The things that have been written, published, or even just written and left for a few months, begin to be like . . . it's like going back to live a part of your life that's already finished. I'd rather live the part of my life that isn't finished, that's going on now.

I don't know if that's a very coercive parallel, so let me think about that. You were a different person before and surely what you did then you did with the self that you were then as well as you could. And for another self, your current self, to go back, it just seems sort of like translating. It's translating from your same language, so it doesn't have those hazards. But it is doing somebody else's work in the words that you would use now. And phrases and pauses.

Is there a point when you start working toward a negotiable poem?

I'll follow this out a little bit. A negotiable poem for me is something that could be sent out into the world, that someone else might respond to. I respond to my own from the very first, you know. My journal entries are fine with me. But every now and then I feel I'm getting something going that begins to have a trajectory that can be tuned for inner reverberation somehow. And that interests me. I tune it up and then I have it for awhile. For instance I have a little folder out there with a whole lot of things that, so far as I'm concerned, are finished, but I haven't yet—except for some of them—felt confident enough or good enough about to send out.

But someone may write to me from a certain magazine. They're interested in a certain kind of thing. Then I read through these things that for me are like characters ready to be sent out, you know, like actors ready to go take a part. And with this magazine in mind I look through them and every now and then I find one that seems to have been written for this magazine. Then I send it out. So it's more like having replaceable parts ready here for magazines. Your magazine needs something. In the extreme it's someone who writes and says I'm having a special issue on the Bible, or we're having an issue to honor Richard Eberhart, or something like that. Do you have anything that would fit? I go through, I find something that could fit, and then send it out. A grotesque idea occurs to me. And that is, in other words, what I've been writing are a whole bunch of gems, but their settings haven't been established by the world yet.

You know if we wanted to sit on this topic of revision we could scare up things forever. As a matter of fact you make me aware that even such changes as change of person, change of tense, they're all sorts of things you can do with a passage. You can decide about the word order and so on, but I feel that the revision that is intense, that gets after what the distinction is between something original or new or artistic, and just sort of shuffling things together, that kind of revision requires of you more than just an ordering, more than just a correcting, and even more than such apparently drastic things as change of person. There's something else going on—a feeling that you're riding the language while you're doing it. I don't want to make it sound elevated, but it's almost like attaining hovercraft potential as you're going through the language. As long as you're down there rowing and the hydrofoils aren't working, when the hydrofoils start working you really feel it.

Does it feel like that when you're writing it the first time?

The first time can have that. But even if I look at my journal pages as I'm going along here, I'm doing a kind of a dream. Down here I begin to shorten the lines because I begin to feel the hydrofoil going, that maybe I'm going to have passages that reinforce each other, groups of phrases, syllables, parts of discourse, and if I look at any of my pages I see how I keep going out, going in, and it's when I begin to feel the hydrofoil part working that I go in. [*Reading from daily writing for 10/7/90.*] "There ought to be a term for the communication that manages to affirm a positive opinion or judgment, but also negates it now, or under present circumstances." This is wide. [*Reading.*] "Only one meadow knows what that winter meant, that winter when Laurie decided her denial." I begin to feel I'm onto something.

In that case it went from something that seemed very prose-like and explanatory to something metaphorical.

That's right. Maybe that's part of what I mean. You're ready to depart. You're ready to set out from shore and trust yourself to the deep in language and that's the revision, that's the area of revision. Revising the other, the information, that's rational, reasonable. Revising or getting with it on the deep is a different process. It's a willingness to trust yourself to what the waves can help you do or something like that. I don't know if that is very helpful. I think what we scared up here, to my surprise . . . maybe we've both felt it, but we've been able to phrase it in such a way as to say, well, there's revision that is the sort of shuffling work, and then there's a kind of revision where you feel yourself attaining to a relation to language that is potential for unexpected things. My impulse is to be rational, dispel a mystery, get rid of that muse that's so distracting. I always feel that we're somehow neglecting something that is right there before us that we can see and then we say, "Oh, that's how to do it. Now I can turn it on anytime." It's not quite turning it on anytime. It's more like coasting into an attitude or attaining enough confidence. It's not even confidence; it's more like fate, kind of fated dancing with discourse. It will lead. All you need to do is follow.

Well, some people think that the idea of the muse is that not everyone can have it. It's just for the artist. But it's not so, is it?

I don't think so. Everyone has those surges of feeling. When you hear people talking, you can tell. Some of the time they're doing the drudgery work of getting to the point and then they take off; they get excited. Or you can just tell they feel they've got it right this time. "Let me try it," they'll say, and they'll try it and then they'll say, "That's it." They've attained that feeling.

So those are good reasons for trying to get students to get in the habit. I mean there are good reasons for having students write every day in the classroom. That it's just not because you've got to do something in the classroom; it's because something might happen to them.

That's right. Those people who feel that you can corral a bunch of human beings in a room and get really serious and do those basic things you have to do and that anything else is just frivolous, I feel haven't heard the news, that there is a possibility for every human being to enter into this reverberation, this mutual feeling with some medium, either music, or in art, or with language. There are those who feel that must be frivolous, because surely we can learn the rules and do it right. Well, you can learn the rules, but to do it, to become airborne, is a kind of a knack. And I don't think you do it by guaranteeing rote learning.

I think you said if there are any rules, they come through the practice.

Yes. It's strange, because the ultimate authority for a rule that ought to be a rule is that it comes from practice. If you don't have that feeling, then all the rules won't be any good.

How about typed poems that don't get sent out? Is it because you lose interest in them? You don't see them as something you want to send out, but that doesn't mean that you don't enjoy them?

I esteem them, would be one way of saying it. It's not that I feel they're mistakes. It's that sometimes you flake a flint and it's useful. I'm looking at something here—"Tourniquet." I like the idea of a poem of that title, so that sort of kept me going, but I don't think I'm going to do anything with it.

Tourniquet

> For days a wound bleeds—it is
> for pity. It is animals unable
> to tell their suffering. It is refugees
> camped in the desert without water or food.
>
> There is no cure. Red springs will
> flow and many storms bring sympathy
> only in rain, or dusty rain. This is
> a world where blood wanders forth.
>
> They can staunch a wound. They can
> turn their eyes away and even forget.
> In green valleys elsewhere the sun will twist
> onward: Day, night. Day, night. Day, night.

Some poems I've typed up don't seem as coercive. Maybe one-fifth of the ones I type up ever get seriously considered. When I type them I feel I'm at the stage where I can have a little more idea of whether they are negotiable, whether they would help a magazine somewhere. There ought to be a quality so there's an experience reading them, and they ought to be somehow salient in content, some coercive content. Here's another I haven't done anything with:

A big ship goes down. There on the bottom
its rooms filled with water keep all their
possessions. They last a long time, dim,
still. A ghost floats those rooms touching
chairs, tables, dishes, and the languid
pages of books that were carefully shelved.

That same ghost often fingers the furniture
at my house, our permanent flooring and walls,
my strong tools at the bench where bird houses
take shape, the pages that scatter on my desk.
That ghost stands at the front window looking
out the way I do at the trees and lawn.

Here under this kind of water all the sunken
ships, and old farmhouses where we pass,
and the houses of everyone we know—all
waver. We touch them and they slide
slowly away, never quite destroyed
but gone thin as a dream in this night, this ocean.

I think I know why that's not going anywhere. I felt it alive
enough to keep pursuing it, those languid pages and sunken
ship and so on, but it turned into something that was just too
neatly leaned against each other somehow. It seemed like the
kind of poem you could plan. It was just too predictable.

*You said something like that one time about "Traveling through the
Dark."*

Yes, I think so. "Traveling through the Dark" seems to me like
a kind of poem you could learn to write. Whereas "Reading with
Little Sister: A Recollection"—I wouldn't know how to learn to
write that. Or "The Little Girl by the Fence at School"—no one
could ever teach me that form. It's a one in a lifetime form, but
it is a form. So with "It Gets Deep" I can't feel the bounce in it,
and I suppose you can't either.

*So it's possible that if you'd written "Traveling through the Dark" re-
cently, it might not have been sent out?* [Laughter.]

Yeah, I suppose that's right. I think what I'm looking for or what really gives me a good feeling, that kind of hydrofoil feeling, is something that surprises me, too.

Of course, you said about the ending of "Traveling through the Dark" that maybe that's where the surprise is.

Yes, I felt OK about that because I didn't predict it myself until I got there. I knew that was the thing to do and when my group said "Don't," that's when I thought "Aha!" When I look at these pages that never went on, I think that what we just said would cover them, except I see one now and then and think, well, maybe so.

For instance, I was looking at this one. It's called "When It Comes."

> Any time. Now. The next minute.
> Years from today. You lean forward
> and wait. You relax, but you don't forget.
>
> Someone plans an elaborate party
> with a banquet, dancing, even fireworks
> when feasting is over. You look at them:—
>
> All those years when you searched the world
> like a ferret, these never happened—your marriage,
> your family, prayers, curses. Only dreams.
>
> A vacuum has opened everywhere. Cities,
> armies, those chairs ranked in the great
> hall for the audience—there isn't anyone.
>
> Like a shutter the sky opens and closes
> and the show is over. The next act
> will deny that anything ever happened.
>
> Your hand falls open. It is empty. It never
> held a knife, a flower, gold,
> or love, or now. Lean closer—
>
> *Listen to me: there isn't any hand.*

Just the way it comes out I still have a kind of an interest. And I like to be fervent: *"Listen to me: there isn't any hand."* It's as if all of those things that are accumulating in an ordinary way suddenly add up to something I have to say.

So that poem has more possibilities than "It Gets Deep"?

The poems that stay interesting to me are ones I feel I haven't conquered. I even have a phrase for this: "Wood that can learn is no good for a bow." Some of my poems can't learn; they're good for a bow. They've got something in them that wasn't predicted. I just feel better about them.

Videotaped for use in *William Stafford: The Life of the Poem* (TTTD Productions, 1992), videocassette. "Tourniquet" (September 18, 1990) is unpublished. "It Gets Deep at Night" (September 4, 1990) and "When It Comes" (September 20, 1990) are in *The Southern California Anthology*, vol. 9, ed. Melissa Hartman (Los Angeles: University of Southern California, 1991), the first poem as "It Gets Deep," in an earlier version. The correct text of "When It Comes" is reprinted in vol. 10 (1993), ed. James Ragan and Richard Aloia.

Whatever the World Gives Me

"The Animal That Drank Up Sound,"
"At the Playground," "Coming Back,"
"The Magic Mountain"

Perspectives on "The Animal That Drank Up Sound"

The Animal That Drank Up Sound

1

One day across the lake where echoes come now
an animal that needed sound came down. He gazed
enormously, and instead of making any, he took
away from, sound: the lake and all the land
went dumb. A fish that jumped went back like a knife,
and the water died. In all the wilderness around he
drained the rustle from the leaves into the mountainside
and folded a quilt over the rocks, getting ready
to store everything the place had known; he buried—
thousands of autumns deep—the noise that used to
    come there.

Then that animal wandered on and began to drink
the sound out of all the valleys—the croak of toads,
and all the little shiny noise grass blades make.
He drank till winter, and then looked out one night
at the stilled places guaranteed around by frozen
peaks and held in the shallow pools of starlight.
It was finally tall and still, and he stopped on the highest
ridge, just where the cold sky fell away

like a perpetual curve, and from there he walked on
    silently,
and began to starve.

When the moon drifted over the night the whole world
    lay
just like the moon, shining back that still
silver, and the moon saw its own animal dead
on the snow, its dark absorbent paws and quiet
muzzle, and thick, velvet, deep fur.

2
After the animal that drank sound died, the world
lay still and cold for months, and the moon yearned
and explored, letting its dead light float down
the west walls of canyons and then climb its delighted
soundless way up the east side. The moon
owned the earth its animal had faithfully explored.
The sun disregarded the life it used to warm.

But on the north side of a mountain, deep in some
    rocks,
a cricket slept. It had been hiding when that animal
passed, and as spring came again this cricket waited,
afraid to crawl out into the heavy stillness.
Think how deep the cricket felt, lost there
in such a silence—the grass, the leaves, the water,
the stilled animals all depending on such a little
thing. But softly it tried—"Cricket!"—and back like a
    river
from that one act flowed the kind of world we know,
first whisperings, then moves in the grass and leaves;
the water splashed, and a big night bird screamed.

It all returned, our precious world with its life and
    sound,
where sometimes loud over the hill the moon,
wild again, looks for its animal to roam, still,
down out of the hills, any time.
But somewhere a cricket waits.

It listens now, and practices at night.

My first impulse, and really perhaps a fully adequate answer, when someone asks me about an apparent pattern in a poem (like the pattern of seasons in "The Animal That Drank Up Sound") is just to agree that I must have done the obvious thing of using a pattern. But lurking somewhere deeper is another and maybe more interesting account. I'll hazard something about that lurking account . . .

In this poem a typical impulse of growth occurred. I started, this time, with a place in mind, Devil's Lake, up in the mountains southeast of Bend, in Oregon. It's a wilderness, a small lake, surrounded by forest and then peaks. And I launched my animal into the place and let it begin to manifest what its hazy origin in my mind, and its accumulating characteristics, evolved—evolved because of the rugged setting, and even some of the syllables in the words that clustered around the developing story, and then the presence (we were camping there) of that steady, silent, bright and mysterious visitor the moon. The moon asked for attention and awe; and all the backdrop moved quietly for attention in my mind. And once I reached—in the tenth line—for "autumn" to help account for how unfathomable it all felt, I was led to rely on seasons for some of the forwarding of the poem.

But yet—if I went back into the trance, maybe a whole different *torque* would begin; maybe the lurking background would crystallize on some other over-arching pattern:—maybe it is all about dominance and rebellion, maybe life and resurrection, maybe fur and rocks, surface of the lake and all that *unsurface* seethe of living and encountering whatever comes . . .

Maybe the details of the writing exert their quiet, powerful energy on my open welcoming trance; and the surge of discovery makes its own course, like a river loosed in a landscape. We look at the river and say, "See, it had a plan." But it did not have a plan, just a readiness to find what the land would offer so easy and ready an element as water, as language and thought mixed and on the move.

When I wrote this poem I'd been up camping in the mountains, a lake outside of Bend, Devil's Lake, just before you get to Elk Lake. A fellow from a YMCA in California told many Indian stories. I was listening to him around the campfire and I decided to invent this animal that drank up sound. I sent it off to the editor of *The Atlantic,* and the editor wrote to me. He wanted to print half of it, which he did. Later an editor of another magazine published the second part.

Mostly little things make poems. In fact, the other thing I was going to say besides just linking whatever you start with onto something that makes it more. Many of us at school were taught that writers or thinkers, people who run the world, they have big thoughts. Sometime I'd grow up and I'd have big thoughts, too. It didn't work out that way for several reasons: one is this—people who do big things don't really have big thoughts. They have little thoughts, but then they add to them. So they pay attention to what they think. If you think something or have an idea, often you think, well, that idea can't be worth anything. No, it doesn't amount to much, but it amounts to something, and then you just put a little bit more with it, and a little bit more. Pretty soon it's big. The good thing about writing is it's a process, it's a way of thinking so that you can start little and end with something bigger.

After *The Atlantic* published Part 1, I met a friend who said, "Bill, what's happening to you? I've been seeing things you've written recently, and they're all so dismal. Terrible things are happening to you. There's some kind of crisis in your life. I wonder what's wrong." And then I realized this. Maybe we're in a time when people are writing all sorts of things, but editors are pessimistic and they are publishing Part 1 and not Part 2.

When I was in Iran, in Tehran—this was in the early seventies—poetry was, maybe still is, very popular, so they were going to have my reading in a big auditorium with two overhead projectors to project the English version and the Persian version so the audience could see both. The translator of my poems came to see me just about the day before the program, and said, "Some of your poems are so political." Well, I thought, could be, but what do you mean? He said, "This one," and he had "The Animal That Drank Up Sound." Standing there in a country where they had censorship and a dictator—the Shah, think about it— they look at my poem: "Who is that animal that drinks up sound in a dictatorship?" It didn't take me long to say to him, "OK, OK, whatever you say." So I didn't read "The Animal That Drank Up Sound."

While our friends circled a campfire at night in the Cascades by Devil's Lake, a friend told stories out of the dark, how everything was quiet and then a sound came nearer and nearer. The children drew together and leaned forward, and I wanted to have a story to tell. From the lake we heard a splash—that's when it came to me, The Animal That Drank Up Sound.

Once an idea like that begins, I urge it on, let it find words and big soft feet or whatever it needs. It can turn aside for awhile and stop, then decide where to go next. If a lake is lapping, I let it in. If a night bird calls, I might even make it louder and more lonely. Whatever the world gives me I welcome and weave it in.

How exciting to have all these adventures in life! If my story can find its way all over and come home just right, then our family will always be together, by some campfire, leaning forward to listen.

Subliminal Elements

At the Playground

Away down deep and away up high,
a swing drops you into the sky.
Back, it draws you away down deep,
forth, it flings you in a sweep
all the way to the stars and back
—Goodby, Jill; Goodby, Jack:
shuddering climb wild and steep,
away up high, away down deep.

If you go far enough back, poems begin, I suspect, with very slight—with subliminal—elements. My own often come from syllables or combinations of them: "*Ours are* the streets *where*" or "In the *late night listening.* . . ." Whole stanzas can catch their way forward by a combination of sound and feeling:

Away down deep
and away up high
a swing drops you
into the sky.

"High" and "sky" are more than rhymes—their *meanings* rhyme.
And I have come to trust the language to bring me more than I
could have hoped for. From its accumulated resonances of
sound and meaning, I derive great bonuses, if I lean forward
and hope.

Almost anything can start the process, and there's a kind of
natural swing to it. This just seemed to be a simple thing to read
to remind myself of what's not just attached to a simple poem,
but maybe to all of them, and maybe to thinking. Maybe to laws,
religion. Just "away up high and away down deep" seems so in-
evitable. The limit I feel as a writer is I trust this. I don't see any
way to get out of this. This is the way we feel things. But I feel
limited in what occurs to me after I get started. That's the limit.
I don't feel restive about the process.

That Trance-like Feeling

Coming Back

Near your face a breath, your dog: "It's day."
Into those dark eyes, receiver wells
responsible for all there is, you fall,
and come back new, brushed by such deep love
the world fades.

The world fades
and brushed by such deep love comes back new.
You fall, responsible for all there is,
those dark eyes, receiver wells
near your face, a breath, your dog. It's day.

I think I can sort of remember that trance-like feeling of fol-
lowing it into the center of the poem and then following the
center of the poem back out by successive steps the way it went
in. Hardly anything edited, a few things changed.

In your revision you changed "divine" to "new." In the daily writing?

No, not on this. Someplace where I typed it probably. At some stage that just dropped out and "new" went in.

Why, do you think?

I have a turmoil of feelings about this. I believe "divine" is nearer the simple-minded way that I really am and "new" is nearer the sophisticated poet I've become. I feel a little guilty about that. I believe if I'd be honest, I'd be a lot worse poet than I am. [*Laughs.*] That's a little bit of fakery. It's sounds as if "divine" is the fakery but "new" is the fakery. "New" is the hard-headed, more cynical, arrived writer.

I think, when I was writing this poem I was so much heart and soul in it, this feeling of receiver wells, you know, eyes as receiver wells that you come back transformed, sort of redeemed, divine, knighted by God sort of thing. But then in the printed version of my poem for the world, not for the transaction between me and God, the printed version just has you "come back new." Even "renewed" is quite a claim, but "divine" is more of a claim, and what I felt was more of a claim. There's a little point I'd like to cling to: maybe to write at least in the way I'm trying to exemplify and trying to be in my life, you need to be so unguarded that you're foolish. The complete abandonment of caution and the "resting in the arms of the loving Lord" sort of feeling is where the impulse comes from, and then in order to get along in the world and not to seem fakey, you fake it. The part sounded too fakey, so I had to fake something that sounded authentic.

One thing I wanted to ask you is if you can say anything about the impulse to come back out of the poem the way you went in.

You mean where that impulse comes from? I don't know. It looks as if it's a poem that has been organized, that goes in and comes out, but as is evident even from the way I wrote it in my daily writing, I don't know why I made that turn and came out. I hadn't done it that way on other poems. There may be a name for this form for all I know, but I hadn't decided to do the form. While I was writing, it suddenly occurred to me. It seemed the right thing to do. I don't think that sounds very helpful. It just seemed right.

It's not in the software of my poem, it's in the hardware of my head.

Maybe the language itself had something to do with the idea of come back divine and the return, and if the world fades does it come back in?

Yeah, if you faded it out you can fade it in. It's day at the end. It's not faded; it's day. The poem came from having a dog that was like this. Leif, a Siberian husky with those blue eyes. I'd be asleep and Leif, a fairly obstreperous dog, was strangely courteous in the early morning. Somehow I'd feel something on my face, and I would wake up, and Leif's nose would be right up there by my face. He wouldn't be saying anything. He was too courteous to wake me up, but his breath would touch my face. I'd open my eyes and there would be Leif looking right at me, and as soon as I would open my eyes, his tail would start, and that sort of feeling is what started the poem.

In this poem, the "brushed by such deep love." Is it a love for animals or that animal, or does it go beyond that animal?

I suppose primarily it was Leif, that look of adoration on his face. I mean, he was really a loving dog, but also in the poem that becomes more universal. I suppose that "brushed" got in there partly because his whiskers were right up here. They're not touching me, but they're right near, and the love that he's showing makes the world fade and then come back new. It's a kind of renewal every morning of the world as a result of this kind of mutuality with the dog. It's also the general deep love there is in the world.

Revisiting "*The Magic Mountain*"

The Magic Mountain

A book opens. People come out, bend
this way and talk, ponder, love, wander around
while pages turn. Where did the plot go?
Why did someone sing just as the train
went by? Here come chapters with landscape all over
whatever happens when people meet. Now
a quiet part: a hospital glows in the dark.
I don't think that woman with the sad gray eyes
will ever come back. And what does it mean when

the Italian has so many ideas? Maybe
a war is coming. The book is ending. Everyone
has a little tremolo in them; all
are going to die and it's cold and the snow, and the clear
air. They took someone away. It's ending,
the book is ending. But I thought—never mind. It closes.

1

You write every day, and if you have standards, you get discouraged, because not every day are you writing *War and Peace*—it's not like that. And why shouldn't our students realize that's a possibility? Just a short time ago I was trying to write, and I always can, because as some people here know, I have my formula, that is, if you feel yourself stalling, if you feel that you're getting writer's block, you just lower your standards and keep going. So I was writing, and I didn't have very much to say, as usual, and I wrote a sentence, one of those genius sentences:

A book opens.

Hmm. Once I wrote that, I wrote,

People come out, bend
this way and that, fight, love, wander around
while pages turn.

Not much genius here: a book opens, people come out, well, that's a pretty bright idea, people come out, and they do this and that. I could have loaded anything into this sentence, just so something's going on. You know. It says,

wander around
while pages turn. Where did the plot go?

That's the next thing I wrote. At this point, this just began to be a certain book. I didn't have a book in mind when I started. But I began to think of a book. "Where did the plot go?" The sort of feeling I'd had when I'd recently read *The Magic Mountain*. You

know, people wander around—where did the plot go? I know
I'm reading a rich book, I'm driving a big Cadillac of a book, I
know that, but where did the plot go?

Why did someone sing just as the train
went by?

Once I'm started, I'm so lazy, once I get something going, you
know, where did the plot go?

Here come chapters with landscape all over
whatever happens when people talk.

You remember this book?

                                        Now
a quiet part: a hospital glows in the dark.
I don't think that woman with the sad gray eyes
will ever come back. And what does it mean when
the Italian has so many ideas? Maybe
a war is coming. The book is ending. Everyone
has a little tremolo in them; all
are going to die and it's cold and the snow, and the clear
air. They took someone away. It's ending,
the book is ending. But I thought—never mind. It closes.

Now, maybe this has a form. It closes. That's a neat way. But
that's what books do. So it didn't take genius.

But what I'm trying to get at is, maybe if I can be forgiving
enough of myself when I'm writing, things will come to me,
even things at the edge of possibility will come to me. And that's
so precious to me that I can't have standards. And if I face a
room full of students, and make them feel "A book opens" is in-
adequate, it's not "Avenge, O Lord, thy slaughtered saints," or
something at the beginning . . . But it's got to be all right, it's
got to be all right to talk, it's got to be all right to write, it's got
to be all right to be like this, the way we all are. That's what I'm
trying to find.

2

I do one of these tremendously creative sentences—"The book opens." Big deal! Did I go get an advanced degree to be able to write things like this? Not much is happening, but then people come out. It's only after it got going that it began to converge with the book I'd just reread, *The Magic Mountain*. It has most of these things in it. "Why did the Italian have so many ideas?" I'm all over the place, but I didn't say I'm going to mobilize my education, I'm going to write a poem about *The Magic Mountain*. Instead I cast myself adrift and see what happens. Pretty soon here comes "*The Magic Mountain*."

3

1) I let myself drift into writing lines that became a poem called "*The Magic Mountain*."
2) In those lines I let pieces of experience come out of a book.
3) The book I then thought of was Thomas Mann's *The Magic Mountain*.
4) That book drifts through scenes that pretend to offer themes and ideas but really orchestrate moods or the settings that create moods.
5) I began to see that art goes directly to the texture of living and is subverted if it accedes to those who delusively think that their lives are essentially goal-oriented and given over to stated purposes.

Every day something keeps me from the main business of my soul.

"The Animal That Drank Up Sound" (1963). Part 1 was published in *The Atlantic Monthly*, part 2 in *Northwest Review*. The whole poem appears in *The Rescued Year* (New York: Harper and Row, 1966) and *The Way It Is* (St. Paul: Graywolf Press, 1998). Commentaries: "My first impulse . . ." (undated); "When I wrote . . . ," from unidentified reading (May 10, 1967); "While our friends . . . ," from daily writing (May 17, 1991). Used with revisions as the author's note for *The Animal That*

Drank Up Sound, illus. Debra Frasier (New York: Harcourt, Brace, Jovanovich, 1992).

"At the Playground" (1971), from *Audience, Stories That Could Be True* (New York: Harper and Row, 1977), *Writing the Australian Crawl* (Ann Arbor: University of Michigan Press, 1978), and *The Way It Is* (St. Paul Graywolf Press, 1998). Commentaries: "If you go far enough . . . ," from *The Christian Science Monitor* (February 21, 1978); "Almost anything can start . . . ," from a reading at Hamline University, St. Paul (March 6, 1976).

"Coming Back" (1986), from *Poetry* and *A Scripture of Leaves* (Elgin, Ill.: Brethren Press, 1999). Commentary: from interview videotaped for use in *William Stafford: The Life of the Poem* (TTTD Productions, 1992), videocassette.

"*The Magic Mountain*" (1991), from *The Way It Is* (St. Paul: Graywolf Press, 1998). Commentaries: "You write every day . . . ," from "A Priest of the Imagination," address given at NCTE conference, Louisville, Ky. (November 1992); "I do one of these . . . ," from a reading at the University of California at Santa Barbara (May 1, 1993).

152

"An Indulgence in Loss"

A Dialogue with Richard Hugo

This interchange between William Stafford and Richard Hugo was taped in a motel room in Albany, Oregon, on March 23, 1973. When published in Northwest Review *in the same year, it was given the title "The Third Time the World Happens."*

A Farewell in Tumbleweed Time

One after another, fish fast over the fence
and quick roll to rebound, lost summer
marshaled her ragged bushy-haired children;
and pell-mell for winter, into our starved light
the west blizzard harried bigger Attila tumbleweeds
driven down what became a canyon
wherever you looked and what stood silvery
gray leaning upward—the part of the storm
you could see, your movable cell, a wild prison.

Our house then, disguised to be any house, outwaited
the storm; our mailbox in sunlight held
level; our gate steadied by shadow performed
a scenario. But into it years came, and then all that
bravery everyone praised good people for
was the wrong thing: nothing changed fast, but moss
muted every brick with its message, while
vines tried to find our grandparents' weaknesses
all up the tall chimney.

I was going to come back some day
after the fragments and I found a new home
and offer to the indifferent air a secret

no one there could use at the time:
about four some winter's day, somewhere
roads don't go, where hills come down,
I'd hold out the unfinished years of our life
and call for the steadfast rewards we were promised.
I'd speak for all the converging days of our town.

Then it would be like the flood of Christmas that
preserved every stone and set all the stars on the hill
where the farm leaned when we came out Main Street
with so much richness we couldn't ever give it away.
But all the rest of this time, after Father died, I
haven't been able to tell anyone half of the things
we carried around in that old car and couldn't say;
and there are people now I couldn't confront, even this
    far,
without dislodging everything in the West.

A new time is here now; I have come back,
and though I speak with less noise
all the little clods lie stunned with effort to remember,
for again it is tumbleweed time; they come to
judge us again. I know that the weakness we blame in
    ourselves
is in the judgment we use: I know what I remember
    wheels
endlessly here to say the same thing. And I know it is time
to cut loose off downwind free
like the eagles that keep the mountains clean.

*I'd like to make some observations about specific poems, Bill, get your re-
action, and let you talk about them. Teaching you, I found a whole
bunch of things. I found much more to love than I had before. A poem
I love is "A Farewell in Tumbleweed Time." Let me read a stanza that
I'm envious of. I wish I had written this:*

I was going to come back some day
after the fragments and I found a new home
and offer to the indifferent air a secret
no one there could use at the time:

about four some winter's day, somewhere
roads don't go, where hills come down,
I'd hold out the unfinished years of our life
and call for the steadfast rewards we were promised.
I'd speak for all the converging days of our town.

You know, that sounds like a Hugo stanza to me.

Well, I noticed you had stolen most of my beautiful . . . [Laughter].
No I think that's just lovely, just beautiful. Am I right about this poem that a lot of it is about stability? For example, in the second stanza you talk about "our mailbox in sunlight held / level; our gate steadied by shadow performed / a scenario." Then there's a fragmentation upon leaving: "I was going to come back some day / after the fragments and I found a new home"—a stability where you assume the fragments would come together. Then, somewhat as in your poem "The Farm on the Great Plains," where the impossibility to recapture "whole selves one would like to hold onto" becomes a problem of infinite human significance, you say here:

and there are people now I couldn't confront, even this far,
without dislodging everything in the West.

I assume that "everything in the West" is everything that is inside the speaker in the poem at that moment of writing . . .

Hmm.

. . . as well as the things external to him that now he's beginning to hang onto, that are now becoming less and less fragmentary as the new home is formed.

Yes, I realize now that a number of those poems are like roving back over an area of experience, putting things to rest, making sure that they're where they're supposed to be, or as near where they're supposed to be as I can make them be. It's not so much tidying up as checking and making sure you've done what you could.

At the end you talk about breaking connections, almost as ultimately as in "The Farm on the Great Plains." The connections are broken for you: "Then the line will be gone." But here in this poem it becomes more an act of the will: "And I know it is time / to cut loose off downwind free / like the eagles that keep the mountains clean." It's as if you were saying you should have flowed all your life like the wind, like the tumbleweed.

Yeah.

But a poem does not start as an abstract idea, and I wonder how much you go back and learn about yourself after the poem is over.

You are probably too generous when you don't want to say I start with an abstract idea, for when you were reading just then I realized that the poem is trying out a fairly standard idea. But even so, it's not a standard idea for the poet till he tries it out. Here in this poem I catch myself saying this fairly common thing: it's time to cut loose and get out, let the next thing happen. So this poem tries out the *feeling* of that kind of standard action. Many of the poems I've written have been like trying out an alternative in life, rather than centering on something I'd bet my life on. I wouldn't bet my life on any one of my poems, but all of them—yeah, yeah.

These connections that you want to break fascinate me because I think they are psychic dependencies on the past rather than just the physical act of leaving. There's no doubt in my mind that the speaker in "The Farm on the Great Plains" is only talking to himself on the farm and that once the connection is broken there is no going back. The telephone line is down, and only the posts that held it, the little incidents of our life that got us from one place to another, that are like markers—the sign posts—are the things that remain. In other words, the isolated experiences. And once the total connection with the past is broken, then you are able to face up to what you know, which I assume is a kind of death.

The Farm on the Great Plains

A telephone line goes cold;
birds tread it wherever it goes.
A farm back of a great plain
tugs an end of the line.

I call that farm every year,
ringing it, listening, still;
no one is home at the farm,
the line gives only a hum.

Some year I will ring the line
on a night at last the right one,
and with an eye tapered for braille
from the phone on the wall

I will see the tenant who waits—
the last one left at the place;
through the dark my braille eye
will lovingly touch his face.

"Hello, is Mother at home?"
No one is home today.
"But Father—he should be there."
No one—no one is here.

"But you—are you the one . . . ?"
Then the line will be gone
because both ends will be home:
no space, no birds, no farm.

My self will be the plain,
wise as winter is gray,
pure as cold posts go
pacing toward what I know.

Umm. Dick, I realize that you read a poem the way you go
through the world. You read this poem and you're visualizing
that landscape. To you, those poles are there, and those lines
are gone. Well, they're gone because you say they're gone.

You *say they're gone: "Then the line will be gone."*

Well, for me, I believe the lines are still there. But when you
go through that poem, you sort of take that landscape away
from me. You just described it abruptly, as if you were seeing it
even more clearly than I saw it—and I wrote the poem!

I take it too seriously.

Yeah, you have too much regard for my poem, Dick. But
there was another thing I was thinking of—physically leaving in
life. That can be done, that is done. But in a poem like that it's
as if I go back in order to check whether I'm ever really going
to be able to go away, and I realize I'm not. You know, every time

I go back I belong there. That past, in some ways—physically—
I can escape it, but in my life I'll never escape it.

*Yes, I know. That's why the poem is written in future tense. It is a
promise of something that probably you'll never be able to fulfill.*

Yeah, that's right. In a way, Dick, what I really want to say in
that poem is: "Because the line will never be gone."

Yes. "My self will be the plain."

That's right.

*But isn't it also about dependency on past selves? "Once we fell sob-
bing to the floor as children, and it worked." And as people, don't we try
to hang onto those selves because they worked once? And isn't growing
up a matter of realizing that those selves won't work any more? And so
the line to them is broken? Finally?*

I don't know. For me it's as if those poems are the substitute
for never having fallen sobbing on the floor. You know, they say:
"When I was a little kid could I leave? Yeah, I could leave. Now
I'm grown up and I come back and say, 'Did I leave? No.'"

*I see. That's funny, because it's always struck me as being, if not a
victory over regression, at least the promise to oneself that one will
finally triumph over regression. Which makes it a very un-Roethke
poem, and I think an important poem. Roethke's attractive to young
people because he is so regressive. And for people, say eighteen or nine-
teen years old, it's a hard time in life. In some ways they want to go for-
ward, but in many ways they're sorry to leave that childhood and in-
nocence that got them by.*

Do you think some of his poems in effect celebrate losing? Is
that why people are attracted to them?

*Perhaps because they celebrate childhood, a time people now regret that
they are beginning to leave; and what you're leaving becomes intensely
attractive. For the same reason men often commit second crimes to go
back to prison—because they really love fondling that bar of soap in a
cell.*

Yeah. Well, that's what I thought you meant by regressive—
when you celebrate something that you know you're going to
have to leave. You indulge in the feeling of losing. And that kind
of indulgence is understandable, but it's regressive.

*You indulge in what you are losing, not the losing of it, but the thing
itself.*

For me, it turns into indulging in the losing. I mean, that's what makes the poetry, that's what gives you the reason to keep on making the poem. It's a celebrating of losing.

I would agree with that completely, except it's a lousy definition of regression. [Laughter.] Well, regression is the wrong word, but I agree with you: it is an indulgence in loss that creates the poem.

That poem you were citing, "A Farewell in Tumbleweed Time," is a kind of indulgence in loss. But I don't like that poem very well.

Oh, that's a beautiful poem! You're out of your mind! That's why you got C on the exam in my Stafford course last quarter, C minus! I'm not going to give you a good grade when you don't like poems like that. Now let's look at that poem we were talking about earlier, "Bi-Focal."

Bi-Focal

Sometimes up out of this land
a legend begins to move.
Is it a coming near
of something under love?

Love is of the earth only,
the surface, a map of roads
leading wherever go miles
or little bushes nod.

Not so the legend under,
fixed, inexorable,
deep as the darkest mine
the thick rocks won't tell.

As fire burns the leaf
and out of the green appears
the vein in the center line
and the legend veins under there,

So the world happens twice—
once what we see it as;
second it legends itself
deep, the way it is.

I think that the little bushes in the second stanza indicate, as in a lot of your poems, that love is of the earth only. Love is a representation, I suppose, of something very natural and of no particular grandiose value. Whereas the legend, the real legend—in this case a verb rather than a noun—is certainly the poetic argument for subjectivity in the interior landscape:

> So, the world happens twice—
> once what we see it as;
> second it legends itself
> deep, the way it is.

But it occurs to me that one might say at the end, "the world happens three times: once, what we see it as; second, it legends itself deep, the way it is; and then the part we'd add in real life, where we'd say, and besides that, it isn't even that way either but some other way . . .

But when you say things like that, you start leaving the poem. Those are footnotes. There's one thing that comes through in your poetry, and it comes through in this poem: to you things can't be real until they have our psychic confirmation; or, if we are old-fashioned, the confirmation of our souls.

Well, maybe the poem says that, but in my life I really want to say the world happens three times: once what I superficially see, second what I do my best to see, and third what I suspect I'll never be able to see it as.

Right. Maybe the better way to put it is that the world happens three times: two of them you can use in poems.

Yeah, the third time is when you take the poem apart and say, Here's the faker inside the poem.

And that third way is the way of the critic.

It's sort of dangerous to look at poems after you've finished them, because then you can out-think yourself. You can use the poem for one step and then make another step.

That's right, but these poems are so good you aren't going to do them any damage.

Ah. Uh. As poems, I hope they survive. But as the best one can do, no.

You talked tonight about poems of despair, and the one you read from the new book was really dismal. But I've found this in your poems earlier.

You mean they are dismal things?

Oh yes, Louis Simpson said that properly read your poems will enrich our lives. A friend of mine who likes your poems very much and wants to write about you, Fred Garber, said, I don't want Stafford enriching my life! What I think he means is, there's more to your poems than an enrichment of life.

Well, don't you have this feeling, Dick, that when you write you can go in any direction you want, that what you write can be intensified up or intensified down?

Yes, and only recently have I come on that feeling.

Winterward

Early in March we pitched our scar,
this fact of a life, in dust;
in summer there was a green alarm,
a foxfire of fear, the distrust
of sighting under a willow tree
a little eggshell, burst.

It was mostly quiet, but threatenings
flared wherever we looked;
in autumn the birds fell to the ground
and crawled away to the rocks;
no sleep at night for anyone,
we stared at a moon like chalk.

Now we hear the stars torn upward
out of the sky; the alarm
shadows us as we run away
from this fact of a life, our home.
Oh winter, oh snowy interior,
rocks and hurt birds, we come.

This poem you've got here, "Winterward," says to me that the small and immediate things normally trigger the poem; and we know that often in science this is how great advancements are made. Sir Alexander Fleming did not cure gonorrhea by sitting in the laboratory thinking, How can I cure gonorrhea? He watched some mold, and that's where we got penicillin. But sometimes because you seem to believe that things are connected, in the small immediate view when something goes wrong, then everything's going to go wrong, like a chain mechanism. In "Winter-ward," the small view is a valid one, but you're sophisticated enough to know that all results from a kind of fear. If the fear itself gets in control, the disasters of the outside world or the exterior landscape magnify themselves and start to become catastrophes. Is that an accurate way of . . . ?

Let me look at that.

I sound erudite because I'm reading from notes.

[*Reads.*]

> Now we hear the stars torn upward
> out of the sky;

Drastic things are really happening here!

Right!

[*Reads.*]

> the alarm
> shadows us as we run away
> from this fact of a life, our home.
> Oh winter, oh snowy interior,
> rocks and hurt birds, we come.

Well, but this is just like one of those excursions, you know. You're sitting around. Which way shall I go? Well, how about into Hell today? OK. Well, sort of jauntily you go as far as you can that day . . .

Wherever the old slough ran. In this case, the old slough is the old slough of words.

And disastrous things happen, but for me there's a kind of exuberance about it. When you write a poem, you sit on the sidelines and watch those disastrous things. It's like experiencing the self-destruct play, *The Death of Buster Quinine.* This is a play by Dick Barnes down at Pomona College. It's a one-time play, because in the last act everything blows up and burns down. So Barnes put it on, and pathetically he says it was great, but now it's gone. So he wants to get some money so as to stage it once more.

You mean he blows up the entire set?

Yeah, everything.

What about the actors?

The actors are giant puppets, and they all self-destruct. Here's poor Buster Quinine up on a cliff, and a wire from way up in the dark comes right down into the center of him (people can't see that wire in the dark), but at the very end a rocket comes—zip!—right into this great big puppet and it just explodes and falls off. You know, you've identified with him, and there he goes. So Barnes wants to stage it once more if he can get some money somewhere to build Buster Quinine again. But he can't have very many people around because it's dangerous. So he can't have an audience—that's another trouble. So a poem is like that, except that the audience is immune, just as the poet is. You can have the death of Buster Quinine right there on the page. All you have to do is turn the page and have it all over again. [*Laughter.*]

Anyhow, I like that poem "Winterward."

I sort of like that, even though it's away back there.

I'm taking this book first [The Rescued Year *(Harper and Row, 1966)*] *because I know a lot of the poems were written earlier than the book that preceded it.*

Some of them were.

Notice some things in the poems. The small things can take comfort, but the big things not. For example, "A horse could gallop over our bridge that minnows / used for shade" [*the opening of "Believer"*].

Yeah, I like that. And then what really endangers that bridge is not the horse galloping but the dog trotting.

That's right:

> but our dog trotting would splinter
> that bridge—"Look down," my father said, and there
> went Buster to break that bridge, but I called him back
> that day:—whatever they ask me to believe, "And
>   furthermore," I say.

Which is a very nice jump, because if I'm getting it right that the smaller, quieter, and slower animal has more effect on the bridge than the horse does, then calling the dog back is symptomatic of a repression of self that leads one, through social insecurities, to join in with the mob: whatever they ask me to believe, and furthermore, I say, *to agree with others to make them feel good.*

That part about *to make them feel good* is where I stall a little bit. They do make extreme claims, but I not only believe what they say, I say *even more,* and believe that too.

Ah, well, I wasn't getting that at all.

Well, my father was telling me something like that in saying that a dog trotting across a bridge is harder on it than a horse galloping. So I see our dog Buster running toward the bridge, and I don't want Buster to bust the bridge. So I call Buster back. And when people tell me these extreme things and think I won't believe them, I say, "And furthermore . . ."

I see. I saw it as a parallel repression of dog and repression of one's own instincts.

Well, what I think about it as of now is: my father tells me something that might be hard for some people to believe. I not only believe him, but I suddenly see that our dog is going to run across the bridge and break it down, so I call him back. So someone else tells me something that they think is going to impose on me; I say, "Not only that . . ." So I guess it's a kind of aggressive acceptance.

I understand.

Is it OK?

Yes, better than what I said. I taught this poem all wrong. I'll raise your grade to C plus. [Laughter.]

It sounds to me as if my poem has flunked. [*More laughter.*] Furthermore . . . [*More laughter.*]

One thing I'm interested in in these poems: you always talk about bonuses of the world, and getting the gifts and being receptive. I know I've told you about the one line that was given to me that was so beautiful I could never write the poem. Beautiful opening line, an old guy said to me, "Harold knew I'd been burned out in the valley." I lost that one. But notice here you say,

> for I understand that the wrong sound weakens
> what no sound could ever save, and I am the one
> to live by the hum that shivers till the world can sing:—

And there's the provision, you see—the gift, the bonus.

Yeah, I like that.

"And I am the one / to live by the hum that shivers till the world can

sing" is almost your creed on creativity, or at least was at one time, if I understand.

Yes, I think I still feel that way.

Another place is in "One Home":

> To anyone who looked at us we said, "My friend";
> liking the cut of a thought, we could say "Hello."

Did you happen to see a movie called McCabe and Mrs. Miller?

No.

Very beautiful film, and I thought you would like it very much, because all the relationships are based not on anything people have in common but simply on need, because it's in a frontier—in the Pacific Northwest—in the mountains, and it's winter, and there's this little town, and the most desperate people get together in it, simply because there are no other people. And when I saw the movie I thought of your line: "To anyone who looked at us we said, 'My friend.'" That is very western. It's interesting to be in New York and meet someone and like them very much; then you meet someone else, and they immediately pick this person apart—with great insight, you know—pointing out, "Ya, but did you notice about this?" And you think, "Yeah." But then you realize—at least I realize—well, I come from Montana, where some guy may be the biggest bastard in the world, but if he has one redeeming quality, he still becomes your friend for life. Because people are so lonely.

Well, in New York friends are disposable. Another comes along every minute.

That's right. People can really pick and choose. Lots of people.

Out here we gotta put up with each other.

That's right. We have no choice. Well, in Oregon it's getting so you don't have to put up with each other. There's a lot of people out here.

The Willamette Valley of Oregon.

Tonight you were saying you would like to live in a world where feelings could be, if not explained, at least appealed to by certain gestures, such as putting a charm on the car for safety. And I link this impulse to that poem ["One Home"]:

> A wildcat sprang at Grandpa on the Fourth of July
> when he was cutting plum bushes for fuel,
> before Indians pulled the West over the edge of the sky.

There, where the natural world is somewhat hostile to just the normal basic needs of the family, such a world becomes comfortable only when it's explained by a kind of childish invention—"before Indians pulled the West over the edge of the sky"—which is a highly imaginative explanation of how limits occur.

Well, yeah, but even in that poem it's almost as if I'm saying, "And furthermore . . ." They tell me a story, and it gets really wild: wildcat after grandpa . . . on the Fourth of July . . . before the Indians pulled the West over the edge of the sky. When they told me those stories, they turned into really great stories.

Great.

My impulse is first to say, "Yes. Say, remember when grandfather used to have to go out and get little tiny sticks of cottonwood to burn?" And pretty soon it's plum bushes. And pretty soon it's wildcats jumping out of the plum bushes. Pretty soon it's on the Fourth of July! [*Laughter.*] My grandpa was really a great storyteller . . .

I know—the Fourth of July. It's a great touch.

That's when things happen in Kansas.

Yeah, but that brings out all kinds of Americana—how our stories become myth. One poem that I really liked, one that you read tonight, called "A Stared Story" . . .

I'm glad I happened on that.

A Stared Story

Over the hill came horsemen, horsemen whistling.
They were all hard-driven, stamp, stamp, stamp.
Legs withdrawn and delivered again like pistons,
down they rode into the winter camp,
and while earth whirled on its forgotten center
those travelers feasted till dark in the lodge of their chief.
Into the night at last on earth their mother
they drummed away; the farthest hoofbeat ceased.

Often at cutbanks where roots hold dirt together
survivors pause in the sunlight, quiet, pretending
that stared story—and gazing at earth their mother:
all journey far, hearts beating, to some such ending.
And all, slung here in our cynical constellation,
whistle the wild world, live by imagination.

In this creating of stories—if I understand the poem right—you're making claim that humanity has a tendency to see all ages except the one they find themselves in as well-ordered, possibly even fascist in nature, but benevolent. For example, in the first stanza, the travelers are feasting in the lodge of the chief. This is a benevolent chief, he has them in to eat. There's a uniformity and order—"over the hill came horsemen, horsemen whistling"—happy perhaps. And there's a military quality about it— "They were all hard-driven, stamp, stamp, stamp"—regular. The causes of things are simply ignored by these people. They are living in an orderly and in many ways a fulfilling way despite the maybe fascistic implications and the military quality. "Into the night at last on earth their mother"—one does not question, one does not worry about the place of mother, one just assumes—"they drummed away; the farthest hoof-beat ceased." And once they're out of the way, then what's holding things is much more tenuous—"Often at cutbanks where roots hold dirt together"—if not tenuous, at least they can be seen and are real and therefore pliable or vulnerable, because roots can be cut and so forth—I mean, now we see what's holding the world together. The world for them was just together, and now by staring we literally bring the truth of this myth of the past into existence.

A philosopher I like—only because he wrote better than most of them—Santayana—said history is nothing but recorded dream. It seems to me that in this poem we are living in a positive way, and the earth is still our mother, but we take far journeys. And although the Indian is the same as modern man, we suffer more anxiety—our hearts are beating, and our constellations become cynical. That is to say, by knowing more or being able to see more about it, we believe in it less and depend on it less as a source of stability. And we whistle too, but we whistle the wild world, and we live by a sort of imagination. We are thrown back to ourselves and whatever moment we are living in. We feel we are being thrown back on our own resources. Another time—we stare that other time into existence when life was orderly, and when there was a benevolence and a provision being made. Here we have to do the providing ourselves through the imagination. Am I in the ballpark?

It seems to me you go right down that poem the way I think back through it; that's the way it goes for me. Those early, primitive people, no matter what happened, it was all done in circumstances that for them were meaningful, and they were part of this drama that was going on.

This is what we believe because we've stared it into the truth.

Yeah, okay. And now we stare at cutbanks, and we start that story. We make it come. And then for ourselves, at the end, we're slung here in this cynical constellation, and we must redeem it somehow by imagination.

But I wanted to ask you something, Dick, as a writer. That line, "slung here in our cynical constellation" came to me as sound, partly. And I don't know if I'd have said it was "cynical" if it hadn't been so handy to have the word-sound "cynical" come after "slung" and before "constellation."

Yeah. The music is flawless.

We must do what we can with sound.

That's right. All truth has to conform to music, even if it doesn't.

In sound, it's not so much how spectacular it is or how hard you hit, but—like Buster and the bridge—it's the cadence. If you hit things at a certain time, you can make great things vibrate. And that's what the dog's soft little feet did.

Here's another poem—"Elegy"—about memories and the memory of deprivation, which apparently is something that you hold onto as a poet: "I hold that memory in both my arms— / how the families there had starved the dogs." Here again are you admitting to falling in love with the source of the poem, which is loss?

In a way. This journey is going with someone who makes vivid for me what's in the world:

> —we walked west
> where all the rest of the country slept.
> I hold that memory in both my arms—
> how the families there had starved the dogs;
> in the night they waited to be fed.
>
> At the edge of dark there paled a flash—
> a train came on with its soft tread
> that roused itself with light and thundered
> with dragged windows curving down earth's side. . . .

Yes, a beautiful description.

But this is all *for* me, at least in the poem. It's there because of someone who took me while the rest of the country slept, and all of these things came alive for us. And even the story of how

168

the families starved the dogs is sort of distanced by being told
to me.

Elegy

The responsible sound of the lawnmower
puts a net under the afternoon;
closing the refrigerator door
I hear a voice in the other room
that starts up color in every cell:
>   Presents like this, Father, I got from you,
>   and there are hundreds more to tell.

One night, sound held in cornfield farms
drowned in August, and melonflower breath
creeping in stealth—we walked west
where all the rest of the country slept.
I hold that memory in both my arms—
>   how the families there had starved the dogs;
>   in the night they waited to be fed.

At the edge of dark there paled a flash—
a train came on with its soft tread
that roused itself with light and thundered
with dragged windows curving down earth's side
while the cornstalks whispered.
>   All of us hungry creatures watched
>   until it was extinguished.

If only once in all those years
the right goodby could have been said!
I hear you climbing up the snow,
a brown-clad wanderer on the road
with the usual crooked stick,
>   and on the wrong side of the mountains
>   I can hear the latches click.

Remember in the Southwest going down the canyons?
We turned off the engine, the tires went hoarse
picking up sound out of turned away mountains;
we felt the secret sky lean down.

Suddenly the car came to with a roar.
And remember the Christmas wreath on our door—
when we threw it away and it jumped blue up the fire?

At sight of angels or anything unusual
you are to mark the spot with a cross,
for I have set out to follow you
and these marked places are expected,
but in between I can hear no sound.
The softest hush of doors I close
may jump to slam in a March wind.

When you left our house that night and went falling
into that ocean, a message came: silence.
I pictured you going, spangles and bubbles
leaving your pockets in a wheel clockwise.
Sometimes I look out of our door at night.
When you send messages they come spinning
back into sound with just leaves rustling.

Come battering. I listen, am the same, waiting.

*I see. I didn't see it as a story but as something you actually happened
onto in this new world.*

Well, it's something we encountered. In a way, it's sort of like
Grandpa cutting plum bushes for fuel and so on. Even the dras-
tic things in the world are vivid, and so it's something precious.

*That's right. That appeals to me especially, because I remember as a
boy—though I've never been able to use it in a poem—during the De-
pression I used to fish in the Duwamish Slough, and when the tide
would go out, there would be bloated dogs in the mud with sacks of rocks
tied around their necks, because people couldn't afford to feed their ani-
mals. During the Depression that's how they got rid of them, and I re-
member that very vividly. A mnemonic irrelevancy, the critics call it, and
let them have their terms, but nevertheless that's what I thought of. A
mnemonic irrelevancy—whoopee!*

One of your memories that got in the way of *my* poem.

Well [laughter], *you have your vivid memories and I have mine,
and your vivid memories in your poems can't help but recall mine some-
times.*

I shouldn't say it's in my poems. In some ways, it's what tugs you anyway. Our memories converge.

Yes, quite often that's true. Also our ways of looking at the world converge. Anyway, you know how poets are: when they're reading they're just thinking.

So you've been populating my books with your ideas.

That's right. Actually, they're not your books anymore—I've taken them over. If I can just get Harper and Row Company to put my name here in place of yours . . .

I know—I'll start writing poems like James Dickey, with gaps in them, and in those gaps you can put your poems. It's what you've been doing anyway, crowding my lines.

I don't mind stealing. I have no pride at all.

The loss, that's established, and the unfriendliness that results in this stanza—"If only once in all those years / the right goodby could have been said!"—the kind of painless and formal departure that is preferable presumably to what really happened, which isn't stated, brings, "I hear you climbing up the snow . . . and on the wrong side of the mountains / I can hear the latches click." This is where things get grimmer, I think, in the poem. No matter how the disconnnections were made, they were always wrong. Disconnection in itself is a wrong.

Yeah. Right.

Unlike "The Farm on the Great Plains," where it promised to be a great right, here it is a wrong. And it wasn't made the right way, formally, properly. And consequently what is left is this aimless wandering figure in an alien world, where "the latches click," and I assume that means the doors are no longer open to him.

Yeah, the goodby is done, and the door is clicked shut. It's all over.

I got hung up in class on that stanza about the motor. I was reading into that, because I know when people didn't have any money they used to turn the key off and let the car roll downhill to save gas.

I thought everybody always did that.

Well, it was always against the law to, but everybody did it during the Depression, and somehow I worked that in as a kind of poverty thing. But reading the stanza, I wonder if there was something wrong with the car, and it was done just to get the car started.

No, actually I was right with you in those old days. It didn't make any difference if it was against the law—you had to have enough gas to get up the next hill.

That's a good guess on my part. You can't make explanations in poems. You leave the art. All you can do is present, as Pound said.

And hope you still have company.

> And remember the Christmas wreath on our door—
> when we threw it away and it jumped blue up the fire?

This is rather involved, given its context in the poem, because what is a gift at one time here is purposely destroyed, although in being destroyed it becomes a momentary gift of a kind of brilliance.

You make me realize that the poem is like—well maybe any poem—it's as if you get going, and in the midst of it you're like a person reaching for this thing and that thing and all sorts of things, just to keep it going. And you think, I can't really make it, but the stanzas are trending, like a collection of memories burned up behind me as I go, passing Christmas, burning up the wreath, going on. But it wasn't intentionally that way. You read it later and say, Now I see what was going on.

It's strange. Tracking through the poem, you make it become a more sustained, coherent elegy than it was for me in the writing. I remember reaching for this thing and reaching for that thing, and it turns out that I happened to be in the midst of things that were incremental—in an elegy.

Don't you find, when you're writing, that after you've written for many many years, you don't even have to go back and make sure that what you put in there next fit? Just because you know it always does, somehow. I mean, when I preach to students, Be arrogant enough to make the next thing belong just because you said it, I don't think that's wrong. I really do think it's just the way our minds work. We cannot say meaningless things. I can demonstrate that you cannot write a meaningless poem.

I do have that feeling myself, Dick. It'll have meaning. You may not like it, but it'll have it.

I believe that too, and I believe that if it fits into the flow of the music of the poem, somehow that's just where it belongs. I have that faith.

It is a kind of faith. That's like a superstition, but I do understand it.

Sometimes I think the will can be kidding itself that this is the imagination, because you might have to go back and do a little more work on the poem, and you really want to go play baseball or something. But I've seen it work out too many times to be wrong.

It's as if sound will help you; sound will keep it going for you. My own feeling is of going forward when writing, and it's surprising how often it works. It's a spooky thing, as a matter of fact.

It is, but it's no more mysterious than the human mind.

I'll say it this way: we can go into the house, and Leif our dog will be running around, and immediately we say something like, Oh—he needs some water. You know, we interpret an action, having associated so long. And I imagine in my poem I come to a line, and it makes a certain kind of yapping sound, and I say, Oh, it needs this line. Oh, it needs some water. [*Laughter.*]

I think that in the best poems phrases do touch each other off. [Laughter.] *Yes, an unfinished poem is a thirsty dog.* [Laughter.]

Give the poor beast some water!

There's a very un-Stafford ending on the elegy poem: "Come battering. I listen, am the same, waiting." The last part of it is not quite in your personal fashion, for you to want the world to insist on itself, to want the real to insist on itself, so much that it becomes loud. You will never do that in the poem yourself, and yet you're invoking the world to do it, to "come battering."

This is an extreme situation. In poetry, the more firmly you have one practice or custom or principle established, the more available it is for some extreme use, some change.

Yeah, yeah, that's right.

So, it's not a matter of how stern your principles are—because no principles can outlast anything—and in a poem you're in the kind of universe in which immovable objects are hit by irresistible forces.

That's good. I noticed that in "Elegy" there's a fanciful accounting of the loss—"I pictured you going, spangles and bubbles / leaving your pockets in a wheel clockwise"—kind of fanciful accounting of what one knows must be terrible, just because the poem was written, and it's an interesting, grandiose way of accounting for things of the imagination. Also, there's an honesty about this in the way the mind does work, and I accept these things with great faith in the poems. The quiet modest

sounds carry the real message: "When you send messages they come spin-
ning / back into sound with just leaves rustling." And then the invo-
cation: don't do that—come back. That's really nice. Gee whiz!

Dick, some people are asking if there are characteristics
peculiar to Northwest poetry.

I think maybe in Northwest poets there is a tendency to use more land-
scape. You don't see W. S. Merwin, you don't see people in the East using
much landscape. Galway Kinnell, to some extent, especially in the
Flower Herding *book. There's just less of the outside world gets into*
Eastern poetry, at least less than I see in the Northwest. I think that we
go outside more than people do in the East. Stanley Moss told me he
hated to call Missoula because nobody was ever home there.

You studied under Roethke, didn't you? That's one question
I was going to ask: are there poets out here in whose work his di-
rect influence is discernible?

I don't see that, and as a matter of fact, his influence on me, al-
though it was considerable, had nothing to do with the way he wrote. I
wasn't particularly attracted to his writing at the time I was studying
with him, but I'm on record as saying what his influence was: that this
outrageous man could take outrageous stances and create something
beautiful out of them. And since I was an outrageous person too, that
gave me a faith that you could be a pretty ridiculous person and still do
something worthwhile or beautiful. But I wasn't influenced by his writ-
ing at all. It was just a matter of seeing another slob who was making a
go of it.

Hmm. In a less spectacular way, that's what we all do for each
other, isn't it?

Uh, yes, perhaps it is. I hadn't thought of that. That's a subtle point
that I'd missed. Yeah.

We're influenced by people, and most of us then try to rar-
efy, angelize, these people. But you do a reverse—you make
them more of a slob, and make them be influential that way.

Well, I don't know. I don't turn them into slobs.

They already are slobs?

Well, I hope so. I'd hate to think that I created them. Anyway, in the
case of Roethke, I use the word "slob" with some affection, but that's
what he was, and that's what I was too. I don't look on my other fellow
poets as slobs, but I do see things. Bill Kittredge says that I see similari-
ties in the ways they take their lives seriously—elements in their lives se-

riously—this is what I see. Not seriously the way most people take them, a totally different kind of seriousness . . .

You mean, take their lives seriously, not the effect of their lives but the elements of their lives?

Yeah, their experiences, if you will, and their relations with the world. Most poets I know are very conservative—and I'm not talking about political conservatism—but they like preservations of relationships with the world. Most poets I know do not want to see the Louis Sullivan buildings torn down in Chicago. It's not a matter of preserving art: it's not that kind of a snobbish attitude.

They just don't want anything to happen, you mean?

They don't want anything to happen. It's what Auden calls the "poetic city." It's a place where the same number of people would always be there doing the same jobs. This would be the ideal place, because I think all poets take their relations with the world very seriously. Now in the case of some of us in the Northwest, the things we love may be swamps. Did you hear Bill Kittredge talk about that alkali thing over at Lakeview? That's a very important thing to him, no matter how much an improvement it might be to fill it in and kill the mosquitoes. In other words, that is a progress that spiritually he couldn't afford: you don't want the old bridge torn down even though it can no longer handle the traffic, though you might momentarily want it when you happen to be driving.

But as a poet . . .

But as a poet you don't want it torn down because then in a way your relations with it are destroyed. In its worst form this attitude results in a kind of sentimentality.

You make it sound as if the writer just wants to go back and breathe over things, just keep them there and talk about them and tell them over.

A kind of psychosthenic dwelling. Yes, and I believe that writers do that as you said earlier. We play back our losses: this is the source of poems. (That's not exactly the way you put it.)

You know, I can't escape that. But when you say it, it makes me uncomfortable.

Me too, because I know it's not healthy. But I also know it happens. Well, I guess it isn't supposed to be healthy, is it? Art isn't.

That's what bothers me, though—I believe it is.

That it is healthy?

I would like to feel that it is. Maybe I'm being sentimental.

You mean that what I'm talking about is a healthy process, or that art is a healthy thing?

Well, I thought maybe art is a healthy process, and that what you are talking about doesn't sound like a healthy process.

It isn't a healthy process. I think it has landed me in trouble twice. I mean real serious psychological trouble. I don't think it is a healthy process, but it was my own fault. I took it too seriously. Literally, I started taking my own poems too seriously. One time I tried to act them out in real life. This is terrible.

Yeah, that's right. Never do that. Poems are tough, but poets are tender. . . .

Dialogue from *Northwest Review* 13, no. 3 (1973), reprinted by kind permission of Ripley Hugo. "A Farewell in Tumbleweed Time" (1963), from *Southern Review* and *The Rescued Year* (New York: Harper and Row, 1966); "The Farm on the Great Plains" (1956), from *Poetry, West of Your City* (Los Gatos, Calif.: The Talisman Press, 1960), and *The Way It Is* (St. Paul: Graywolf Press, 1998); "Bi-Focal" (1950), from *The Nation, West of Your City* (Los Gatos, Calif.: The Talisman Press, 1960), and *The Way It Is* (St. Paul: Graywolf Press, 1998); "Winterward" (1953), from *Nimrod* and *The Rescued Year* (New York: Harper and Row, 1966); "A Stared Story" (1953), from *Poetry Northwest, Traveling through the Dark* (New York: Harper and Row, 1962), and *The Way It Is* (St. Paul: Graywolf Press, 1998); "Elegy" (1952), from *Western Review, Traveling through the Dark* (New York: Harper and Row, 1962), and *The Way It Is* (St. Paul: Graywolf Press, 1998).

Just Thinking

Got up on a cool morning. Leaned out a window.
No cloud, no wind. Air that flowers held
for awhile. Some dove somewhere.

Been on probation most of my life. And
the rest of my life been condemned. So these moments
count for a lot—peace, you know.

Let the bucket of memory down into the well,
bring it up. Cool. Cool minutes. No one
stirring, no plans. Just being there.

This is what the whole thing is about.

"Just Thinking" (1993), from *The Way It Is* (St. Paul: Graywolf Press, 1998).